RECIPES FROM
LE ROUZET
An English Cook in France

Sold in aid of Age Unlimited

RECIPES FROM
LE ROUZET

An English Cook in France

CATHY GAYNER

For my Pa, to whom I owe absolutely everything.

Published in 2021 by Age Unlimited
Avebrick House, Pewsey
Wiltshire SN9 5NT

Charity No.1137423
ageunlimited.org.uk

ISBN 978-1-5272-7746-5

Printed and bound in Italy by L.E.G.O.
Colour Reproduction ALTA London

Project Editor: Henrietta Nettlefold
Editor: Fiona Duncan
Photographer: James Murphy
Additional photography:
Lucia Lowther (pages 36 & 80), Maggie Wilson (page 6)
and John Gayner (page 191)
Food stylist: Jan Smith
Prop stylist: Penny Markham
Designer: Smith & Gilmour

Foreword

The first time I caught sight of my future husband, Richard, he was sitting on the skeleton of the roof of a huge barn in a field in the middle of nowhere, having stripped it bare of its traditional Roman tiles.

With the help of any willing person he could find, Richard was restoring an old farmhouse and barn in Southwest France and when I arrived amongst a group of his friends, it was all extremely basic – one dangling light bulb and one standpipe, Lilos for beds and absolutely no privacy.

But despite all this, despite the dirt and hard work and the complete lack of comfort, that is when my love affair with the house (and its owner) began – and love affair it still is nearly 50 years later. Every time we turn into the drive my heart lifts. The house, barns and tower are made of dazzling white limestone, there are wonderful views across the valley, the fields are full of wild flowers and butterflies, the dark skies twinkle, the nightingales sing almost too loudly and the little red squirrels sound like tap dancers as they skip across the roofs. To me, it is heaven.

It is also one man's life work and since, wherever possible, Richard has undertaken the manual labour himself, it is a very personal and touching legacy for our sons and their families. John and William spent their summers at Le Rouzet surrounded by a never-ending stream of friends, turning this peaceful place into a riotous holiday camp – football and cricket by day, partying by night and no neighbours to complain of noise or bad behaviour. Richard played the parts of chauffeur and sommelier, while I was laundry maid and cook.

Life at Le Rouzet revolves around food and the recipes on the following pages are, for me, a diary reflecting what we ate, reminding me of long meals, of laughter and of happiness, shared with family and friends. And now it has come full circle and I watch with huge pleasure as the grandchildren climb the same trees, play the same games and eat the same things as their fathers did before them.

Cathy Gayner

About Le Rouzet

Three things happen when you get *there*.

First, you are greeted with smiles and hugs the depth and width of oceans. Then, a glass of cold crisp sparkling wine appears, magically. Next to it, a plate – thinly sliced cuts of the local saucisson, thick with pepper and studded with walnuts. Finally, you breathe.

Scoring an invitation to Le Rouzet is as thrilling as discovering a golden ticket to Willy Wonka's Chocolate Factory. And, for those of us unaccustomed to deploying the word "no", almost certainly as fattening.

In simple terms, Le Rouzet is a greatly loved family home perched on a remote hillside in Southwest France. Flanked by fields of sunflowers and fragrant lavender, its ancient central barn and sun-dappled outhouses are surrounded by medieval villages of outrageous beauty and charm.

For those lucky enough to get the call-up, Le Rouzet – from the Latin for "rose" – evokes much more than a sense of place.

There are lazy days in hammocks, spent reading a book plucked from the bulging house library, which spans works from Goscinny to Gore Vidal. And there are bucolic walks in flower-strewn countryside, accompanied by the dance of bright blue butterflies and the comforting hum of busy crickets.

Then there's the market day visit to Montcuq, the local village, where you are assaulted by a riot of colours, the clink of demi-bière glasses and the reassuring clack of boules. There are glistening rows of sun-ripened tomatoes and perfect plump peaches; endlessly imaginative concoctions involving goose and duck; cauldrons of bubbling cassoulet, and breads and cheeses of infinite shape and hue. But all of this is just a sideshow to the main event.

Once you have unpacked your car and taken a dip in the azure infinity swimming pool that overlooks a valley of Cézannic magnificence, the serious work begins.

For the heartbeat of Le Rouzet is Lunch, served outside at a table that can seat 20 guests, as it often does.

Lunch is not lunch as you know it. It requires discipline and management. God forbid that you have not been in training.

For the next two hours (and often longer), you will be presented with a celebration of love, of fun, of joy, of connection and of food that represents the very best things you can share in the countryside with family and friends.

To start, perhaps, there will be a plate of plump radishes served with salted butter. There will be two pâtés for you to consider. Here, a chunky pâté de campagne, rich with duck liver and pork shoulder, there, some rillettes de porc, its fat oozing through the caringly shredded meat.

If you haven't already, you must choose which of the two varieties of local bread you wish to employ or whether, like most around the table, you will succumb to both.

There will be air-dried hams and plump farmhouse saucisson that celebrate the best things about pork and pistachio, and perhaps a thinner sausage redolent with truffle. To accompany them: two, three or even four salads, changed daily to arouse the appetite and sustain interest. Today, perhaps, a glistening chicory salad strewn with shards of crispy bacon and walnuts. In contrast, a bowl of finely grated carrots, golden, radiant, served with pungent, garlic-infused olive oil.

Your nostrils are alerted to newcomers to the table. A tart arrives. Rich, buttery, billowing puff pastry triumphantly holding a mountain of local goat's cheese, leeks and discs of fiery chorizo. Then there's the brace of farmhouse chickens, barbecued over coal and wood, their skins burnished, blackened, crisp and smoky. Perfect for trawling through a bowl of salsa verde, astringent with parsley, basil, mint and capers.

There are now further decisions to be made. There is a cheese board. It has six different species. Your eyes may settle on a slice of the pungent local crottin or perhaps you are taken by the Bleu des Causses, produced from cows which graze on the limestone plateaux of the Dordogne Valley.

By this stage, the first timers are regretting overdoing it on the bread. They can be forgiven. The bread alone was good. Very good. But that's novice. It is nothing short of vital that you pace yourself; the game is still afoot.

To sweeten the palate, there is now a chocolate and salted caramel tart, gooey in the middle and richer than the Sultan of Brunei. To counteract, like a well-placed chess piece, is homemade ice cream, discreetly flavoured with vodka and perhaps embellished with passion fruit or honeycomb.

So far, your glass has been regularly refilled with a floral white or perhaps a Vin de Cahors, made just a few kilometres away.

But your host, Richard, has just made new suggestions. A glass of Armagnac? Or perhaps the local Marc? Or, maybe, just maybe, what about the merest sniff of La Vieille Prune?

As you sink gently, then heavily, into your chair, feeling warm and in love with life because *that's what this food has done to you*, you are now imagining how a culinary odyssey of this scale would not only require a team of three chefs but also a kitchen porter of Herculean strength and endurance.

You'd quite understandably visualise a brigade of sweating, sinewy Gordon Ramsay types swearing at each other as they plated their dishes.

Not so. For all of these truly good things have been lovingly sourced, paired, sliced, diced, whisked, baked, roasted, chilled, grilled, fried, frozen, blended, married, marinated and plated by just one person.

One slight, softly spoken and supremely talented cook called Cathy. It is whispered, jealously, amongst greedy folk that she has never served Richard the same menu twice.

For, like all the best cooks, Cathy is naturally inquisitive, open to new ideas and most importantly, to new tastes.

The result of this curiosity is a lifetime of recipes tried and tested, with thousands of notes (in her exquisite italic handwriting) about what has worked, and what needs improving.

In your hands you have the distillation of this culinary odyssey. A parade of greatest hits from the best cook I have had the privilege of knowing. And even if you never manage to bag one of those Willy Wonka Golden Tickets, you can now recreate the Chocolate Factory in your own home.

And that was just Lunch. Dinner is yet to come…

Justin Gayner

LUNCH
SALADS

In an ideal world, I would live on salads. They have come a long way from the limp lettuces and tasteless tomatoes of my childhood, and are now beautiful, bursting with different tastes and textures. At lunchtime, our long outdoor table, under its canopy of passion flowers, is laden with bowls and plates of multi-coloured salads; it looks, I hope, like a feast.

Instant Salads

Lunch at Le Rouzet tends to be either a tart of some description or a selection of salamis and salads. It is, of course, time consuming to put together the number of salads you need to make lunch look like a feast, so it's a good idea to have a few that you can rustle up in an instant. Some of these salads are complete cheats; all of them are very quick and good for bulking up the display on the table.

TOMATO AND EGG SALAD

Use one tomato and one hard-boiled egg per person. Slice the tomato from the top to the bottom, but not quite all the way through, and slip a slice of egg into each cut. Dollop on some thick homemade mayonnaise (see page 172) and sprinkle with parsley.

CARROT SALAD

If you are in France, buy a large tub of grated carrot from any supermarket. Stir in a large clove of crushed garlic and a splash of good strong olive oil. Decorate with capers.

CELERIAC SALAD

You can buy perfectly good celeriac remoulade in any French supermarket. All you really have to do is to add a large spoonful of Dijon mustard, but if you have time, chop up some capers and cornichons and add these and some parsley to the mixture. If you then decorate it with jambon de Bayonne or smoked salmon, it looks as if you've taken much more trouble than you have.

CHICKPEA SALAD

Open a tin of chickpeas and make a strong mustardy vinaigrette, to which you add a large handful of chopped parsley.

FENNEL SALAD

Slice some fennel as finely as you can (one good-sized bulb will do for three people). Put it in a dish with a good splash of olive oil and a lot of lemon juice and decorate generously with shavings of Parmesan.

MUSHROOM SALAD

You need good firm mushrooms. Slice them very thinly and add a surprising amount of good strong olive oil and lemon juice. The mushrooms soak up the juices in an extraordinary way, so use more than you think. Finely slice a red chilli, chop some parsley and add these to the mixture. Finally decorate with shavings of Parmesan.

BACON AND WALNUT SALAD

All you need for this is some chicory to which you add fried croutons, crispy lardons and toasted walnuts. The vinaigrette needs to be sharp and I make it with cheap olive oil and red wine vinegar.

FETA AND SALAMI SALAD

A good way of using up little bits of salami. Mix whatever you have with chopped tomatoes and crumbled feta. Serve on a bed of shredded lettuce and dress with a sharp vinaigrette.

FRENCH BEAN AND NEW POTATO SALAD

Halve the potatoes and cook both vegetables until just tender. While they are still warm, toss in homemade pesto (shop-bought pesto will not do for this). To make pesto, whizz up a bunch of basil, stalks and all, a clove of garlic, a handful of pine nuts, about 100g of Parmesan and enough olive oil to make a sauce rather than a paste. Season generously. As an alternative you could substitute coriander or parsley and walnuts.

POTATO SALAD

Cut the potatoes (any kind of potatoes will work but salad potatoes would be my preference) into even-sized chunks and cook. Drain and immediately stir in some crème fraîche and lots of seasoning. Decorate with chives.

MELON AND ROCKET SALAD

Cut the melon (any kind will do) into chunks and toss it with lots of rocket in a light vinaigrette dressing.

COURGETTE AND BASIL SALAD

Slice the courgettes thickly lengthways and toss in oil. Cook them on a ridged griddled pan or on a barbecue until they have dark stripes on each side. Then layer the courgette slices with spoonfuls of ricotta, lemon zest and basil. Decorate with shavings of Pecorino.

MOZZARELLA AND MELON SALAD

For one cantaloupe melon cut into chunks, you will need 6 slices of Parmesan and one ball of good-quality mozzarella torn into bite-sized bits as well as a handful of rocket. Toss in a dressing of 2 tablespoons of lemon juice and 4 tablespoons olive oil.

AUBERGINE SALAD

Cut an aubergine or two lengthways into thick slices and brush each side with olive oil. Season with salt, pepper, garlic and thyme and cook at 220°C/Fan 200°C/Gas 7 for 20 minutes, until golden. Arrange on a dish and scatter over crumbled feta, toasted pine nuts and chopped mint.

SQUASH SALAD
Peel the squash and cut it into even-sized chunks. Drizzle with oil and roast at 200°C/Fan 180°C/Gas 6 till tender and beginning to char at the edges. Then toss the roasted squash with watercress, crumbled feta, toasted walnuts and a walnut and lemon dressing. Scatter pomegranate seeds over the top.

WATERMELON SALAD
Cut the flesh of the watermelon into thin slices, finely slice a chilli and scatter it over the top of the watermelon. Add crumbled feta and a small handful of torn mint leaves. Drizzle over a little olive oil.

BROAD BEAN AND PATA NEGRA SALAD
In an ideal world I would always use these two wonderful ingredients, but because preparing the beans is time consuming – they need not only podding but skinning – and in France I have no access to Pata Negra, I often replace the broad beans with soya beans and the Pata Negra with the best prosciutto I can find. The result is still delicious. For two people, tear up 60g of prosciutto and add 120g of uncooked soya beans. Combine with a small clove of crushed garlic, a tablespoon of olive oil and a splash of sherry vinegar and mix thoroughly. This makes a great lunchtime salad and an equally good first course for dinner.

Crispy Garlic Salad

SERVES 6 AS PART OF A SELECTION OF SALADS

Don't be put off by the number of garlic cloves. This is a good way of making a plain green salad much more interesting.

2 Little Gem lettuces
a large pack of
  beansprouts
1 bunch of spring
  onions, finely sliced
10 garlic cloves
3 tbsp groundnut oil
30cm piece of fresh
  root ginger, grated
2 tsp Chinese five-
  spice powder

Dressing
2 tbsp lemon juice
1½ tbsp soy sauce
1 tbsp honey
2 tbsp sunflower oil
2 tsp sesame oil
3 good pinches of
  chilli powder

Cut each lettuce into 8 segments and mix with the beansprouts and spring onions.

Chop the garlic finely and fry in the groundnut oil until it is brown and crispy.

Add the Chinese five-spice powder and the ginger and cook for 1 minute.

Mix the dressing, add it to the salad and top with the crispy garlic.

Patatas Bravas

SERVES 4 AS PART OF A SELECTION OF SALADS

*This is a useful recipe, as you can make the sauce
a couple of days ahead.*

500g potatoes (any
variety will work)
2 tbsp olive oil
150g cooking chorizo
(use the spiciest one
you can find)
400g tin of chopped
tomatoes
4 tbsp balsamic
vinegar
2 tsp smoked paprika
2 tsp caster sugar
salt and pepper
aïoli, to serve

Cut the potatoes into even-sized chunks,
drizzle with oil and roast at 220°C/
Fan 200°C/Gas 7 for 20 minutes.
　　Peel and roughly chop the chorizo.
Pour the tomatoes into a saucepan and add
the vinegar, paprika, sugar, salt and pepper.
Simmer gently for 15 minutes and then add
the chorizo. Simmer for another 5 minutes.
Check the seasoning and add more to taste.
Once the potatoes are golden and crispy,
take them out of the oven, put them on a
serving dish and pour over the tomato sauce.
　　Serve with aïoli.

Nota Bene
You can make aïoli by adding crushed garlic
to homemade mayonnaise (see page 172).

Cauliflower Salad

SERVES 6 AS PART OF A SELECTION OF SALADS

*I love this salad and have been cooking it for about 40 years,
but our boys and their guests gave it a wide berth till they were
well into their teens. If you are going to make it in advance,
keep the breadcrumb mixture apart from the cauliflower
and warm it all through just before serving.*

1 medium cauliflower
110g fresh fine
 breadcrumbs
6 tbsp olive oil
2 garlic cloves,
 thinly sliced
6 anchovy fillets,
 chopped
1 red chilli, deseeded
 and finely sliced
1½ tbsp capers
12 black olives, stoned
 and chopped
salt and pepper

Break the cauliflower into florets and cook
in boiling water for 5 minutes. You want the
cauliflower cooked but al dente. Drain.

Heat the oil in a pan, add the breadcrumbs
and cook for about 5 minutes until they are
beginning to turn crispy. Then add the garlic
and cook for a moment or two, taking care
that the breadcrumbs don't burn.

Add the cauliflower and all the other
ingredients to the pan, season and stir
to warm through.

Roasted Peppers

SERVES 6 AS PART OF A SELECTION OF SALADS

*This is a beautiful salad that adds colour to any table. I also
serve it as an accompaniment to Cod in Seconds (see page 126).*

3 red peppers
3 yellow peppers
3 tbsp strong olive oil
1 tbsp balsamic
  vinegar
1 large garlic clove,
  crushed
2 tsp capers, rinsed
salt and pepper

Cut the peppers in half and deseed them.
Place them on a baking tray and cook at
220°C/Fan 200°C/Gas 7, for about 20 minutes
until beginning to char. Then put the peppers
in a plastic bag and leave them to cool.

In a bowl, mix the oil, vinegar, garlic and
a good amount of seasoning.

Peel the peppers and keep any of the juices
in the bag to add to the dressing. Slice the
peppers into strips, toss in the dressing and
any pepper juices, then scatter over the capers.
If you have any basil, a few torn leaves on
top of the salad is a good idea, but not
absolutely essential.

Red Pepper Vinaigrette

SERVES 4

*There are many versions of this dish, but I make no apologies
for including it in this book because it makes the very prettiest
of salads as well as a fine first course for dinner. Don't be put
off by the quantity of vinaigrette: it is absolutely necessary
and disappears in the most extraordinary way.*

4 roasted red peppers,
  peeled (see page 24)
vinaigrette, made
  with 3 tbsp red
  wine vinegar and
  9 tbsp olive oil
4 hard-boiled eggs
10 anchovy fillets
2 tbsp capers, rinsed
2 tbsp finely chopped
  parsley
salt and pepper

Arrange the peppers on a large dish, season
well and pour over the vinaigrette.

Separate the yolks from the whites of the
eggs, crumble the yolks and finely chop
the whites.

Decorate the dish with the eggs and the
anchovies and sprinkle over the parsley and
capers. Serve with lots of bread to mop up
the juices.

Frankfurter & Potato Salad

SERVES 4

Even if you think you don't like frankfurters, I urge you to try this excellent salad. At Le Rouzet, all ages tuck into it with enjoyment and I am constantly asked for the recipe.

500g waxy potatoes, cut into chunks
10 good-quality frankfurters, cut into quarters
a bunch of spring onions, finely sliced
50g parsley, roughly chopped
1 heaped tbsp Dijon mustard
2 tbsp red wine vinegar
5 tbsp olive oil
salt and pepper

Cook the potatoes in boiling salted water until tender, adding the frankfurters for the last 5 minutes (this will be enough to heat them through).

Mix the spring onions with the parsley, mustard and vinegar and beat in the oil to make a thick dressing.

Drain the potatoes and frankfurters and immediately add them to the dressing. Make sure the chunks of potatoes are not too big: you want each one to be properly coated in the dressing.

Pile into a bowl and serve warm.

Two Aubergine Salads

*Gleaming like a guardsman's boots and with a slightly sinister
beauty, a pile of aubergines looks utterly irresistible – but once
cooked, what an anti-climax their appearance is. However,
these recipes, both very different, celebrate the versatility
of this wonderful vegetable.*

SALAD ONE

Cut aubergines into rounds about 5mm thick and brush
with olive oil and garlic.

Roast at 200°C/Fan 180°C/Gas 6 for 10 minutes.

Remove from the oven and sprinkle a bit of Parmesan
over each slice, then top with a slice of tomato.

Lower the oven temperature to 190°C/Fan 170°C/Gas 5
and bake for another 15 minutes. Finish by sprinkling over
a bit more Parmesan and serve warm or at room temperature.

SALAD TWO

Halve 2 aubergines and score them deeply in a criss-cross pattern.

In a food processor, whizz up half a teaspoon of Sichuan peppercorns, 20g of fresh root ginger, 2 red chillies, 2 tablespoons of tomato purée, 2 tablespoons of runny honey, 1 tablespoon of soy sauce, 1 tablespoon of sunflower oil and 2 tablespoons of water.

Pour the paste on to the cut side of each aubergine.

Cover the aubergines with foil and roast at 200°C/Fan 180°C/Gas 6 for 30 minutes.

Remove the foil, scatter over a handful of sesame seeds and roast for another 30 minutes. Finally, dribble over some sesame oil and sprinkle with thinly sliced spring onions.

Radicchio Salad

SERVES 4

I love this salad but I do realise that it may be thought a little odd. It's a strong hearty dish, more Italian than French, and useful amongst a selection of salads at lunchtime.

2 heads of radicchio
2 large garlic cloves, crushed
2 x 400g tins of haricot beans, drained and rinsed
4 tbsp finely chopped parsley
1 dessertspoon capers
200g black olives, pitted (don't use ones already pitted as they seldom taste as good as they should) and roughly chopped
100g Parmesan, shaved
olive oil and white wine vinegar
salt and pepper

Cut each radicchio into 8 segments, trying to keep each bit attached to the core. Cook on a griddle pan until lightly charred on each side and transfer to a serving dish. Drizzle over some olive oil and season.

Stir the garlic into the beans and season generously. Add 4 tablespoons of olive oil and then vinegar to taste.

Add the parsley, capers and olives to the beans and spoon the mixture around the radicchio. Finally scatter over the Parmesan shavings.

Potato & Parsley Salad

SERVES 6 AS PART OF A SELECTION OF SALADS

*For this I use the cheapest supermarket jambon de Bayonne
that I can find because the French don't produce rashers of bacon.
Whatever you use, you want to end up with something very crispy.*

12 medium waxy
potatoes, cut
into quarters
4 slices of prosciutto
or 4 slices of smoked
streaky bacon
2 tsp red
wine vinegar
4 tbsp olive oil
3 tbsp chopped
flatleaf parsley
2 spring onions,
chopped
salt and pepper

Boil the potatoes until they are cooked.

Cook the prosciutto or streaky bacon in a
hot oven (200°C/Fan 180°C/Gas 6) for about
10 minutes until very crisp, then crumble them
into pieces.

Mix the vinegar and oil together, season and
pour over the potatoes while they are still warm.

Stir in the parsley, the spring onions and
the bacon.

Bulgur Wheat Salad

SERVES 6-8

This accommodating salad improves for being made a couple of hours in advance but sadly, it won't last until the next day, as the nuts go soggy.

350g bulgur wheat
6–8 tbsp olive oil
2 tbsp tamarind paste
juice of 1 lemon
5 tbsp tomato purée
1 tsp ground cumin
1 tsp ground coriander
½–1 tsp chilli flakes, depending on your taste
150g walnuts, toasted and roughly chopped
150g hazelnuts, toasted and roughly chopped
60g pine nuts, toasted
a large bunch of parsley, chopped
salt and pepper

Cook the bulgur wheat according to the instructions on the packet. While it is still warm and will soak up the flavours, stir in the oil, tamarind paste, lemon juice, tomato pureé, cumin, coriander, chilli flakes and seasoning.

Just before you want to serve the salad, add the nuts and the parsley and mix together thoroughly.

Nota Bene
Whenever you are toasting nuts, wait until they are cool enough to handle, then try to rub off as much of the skins as you can – it's a bother but it's worth it.

Couscous with Herbs

SERVES 4

It is very difficult to find coriander in Southwest France, but in an ideal world, I would add 20g into the mixture of herbs that I use for this recipe. When cooking couscous, I always add a stock cube to the boiling water to give it a bit of extra taste.

150g couscous
1 chicken or vegetable
  stock cube
½ tsp ground cumin
50g shelled pistachios,
  toasted and
  roughly chopped
6 spring onions,
  finely sliced
1 green chilli,
  deseeded and
  chopped
a big handful of
  rocket or watercress
juice of 1 lemon
salt and pepper

Herb paste
20g parsley
20g tarragon
20g dill
20g mint
100ml olive oil

To make the herb paste, whizz the herbs with the oil in a food processor.

Put the couscous into a bowl with a chicken stock cube, cover with boiling water and make sure the stock cube has dissolved. Cover with cling film and leave until the couscous is tender. When it is ready, add the herb paste and all the other ingredients, season and stir well.

Couscous & Garlic Salad

SERVES 8

This hearty, glowing red salad came about because one kind guest returned from the market many years ago with an armful of garlic and it seemed unappreciative not to use as much as I could.

350g couscous
1 chicken or vegetable stock cube
1 head of garlic
2 tbsp harissa
4 roasted red peppers, peeled and cut into lengths (see page 24)
olive oil
lemon juice
salt and pepper

Put the couscous into a bowl with a stock cube, cover with boiling water and make sure the stock cube has dissolved. Cover with cling film and leave until the couscous is tender.

Separate the garlic cloves (don't bother to peel them at this stage) and cook them in boiling water for 5 minutes. Then pop them out of their skins and cook them very slowly in olive oil until they are brown and soft.

Stir the harissa into the couscous, followed by the peppers and the whole garlic cloves, including their cooking oil. Finally add a bit more olive oil and lots of lemon juice until you get the taste and consistency you want.

LUNCH
TARTS

I find anything made with pastry very difficult to resist and a tart, which fills the kitchen with a wonderfully inviting smell, is a better summons to lunch than any bell rung by me. (We do have a splendid bell outside the kitchen which I have rung repeatedly over the years but with absolutely no effect on small boys engrossed in one game or another.) Tarts are incredibly useful – a lot of the work can be done in advance – and on a hot day, they are infinitely more appetising than salami and rillettes melting on the plate in front of one.

Red Onion Tarte Tatin

SERVES 6

Ready-rolled puff pastry is too thin for this recipe, so use the kind of pastry that's sold in a block. I always buy pastry that has extra butter in it, but if you can't find any, simply roll out the block of pastry, spread it with butter, fold it over and roll it out again, ready to use.

30g butter
1kg red onions, cut into 2cm slices
2 tbsp caster sugar
60g sundried tomatoes, roughly chopped
225g frozen puff pastry, defrosted

Melt the butter in a frying pan big enough to hold the onion slices in one layer.

Add the onions, sprinkle half the sugar over them and season. Pour in enough cold water to barely cover the onions.

Bring to the boil and simmer for about 30 minutes or until the onions are tender and the water has evaporated, leaving a sticky glaze.

Butter a 23cm cake tin really well and sprinkle it with the remaining sugar. Scatter the sundried tomatoes evenly over the base and then arrange the onions on top as neatly as possible.

Roll out the pastry thinly and lay it over the onions, tucking the pastry in around the sides.

Cook at 220°C/Fan 200°C/Gas 7 for 30 minutes until the pastry is golden. Cover the tin with a large plate and carefully turn it upside down and on to the plate. The onions will be on the top.

Leek Tart

SERVES 6

This is our sons' favourite tart and has been for most of their lives. However, nowadays, I suspect it may be nostalgia, rather than taste, that makes it so important a part of every holiday.

Pastry
Use a 320g pack of the ready-rolled puff pastry you can buy in supermarkets, but make sure it's the kind with extra butter

Filling
100g butter
6 leeks, cut as thinly as a £1 coin
1 x U-shaped chorizo, the strongest you can find, cut into 1cm slices
1½ goat's cheese logs, cut into thick slices

Line a 23cm tart tin with the pastry, tucking the extra bits round the sides to make them stronger.

Cover the pastry with a piece of baking parchment, fill it with baking beans and cook it at 200°C/Fan 180°C/Gas 6 for 20 minutes. Remove the baking parchment and the beans and return the pastry to the oven for another 5 minutes to make sure the bottom isn't soggy.

Melt the butter in a large pan and cook the sliced leeks very slowly with the lid on. This will take about 15 minutes.

Tip the leeks on to the cooked pastry, followed by the chorizo and the goat's cheese. Return to the oven and cook for another 15 minutes or until the cheese is golden.

Garlic & Bacon Tart

SERVES 6

You can freeze this tart up to the point of pouring in the cream and egg mixture.

Cheese pastry
110g butter
140g plain flour
30g strong Cheddar, grated

Filling
3 heads of garlic
3 tbsp olive oil
9 rashers of smoked bacon, chopped
1 egg and 2 extra yolks
100ml cream
salt and pepper

Put all the ingredients for the pastry into a food processor and mix until the dough forms a ball. Press the dough into a 23cm tart tin with a removable base (the pastry will be thin but that is what you want). Prick really thoroughly all over, even up the sides (this will prevent shrinkage), then chill in the fridge.

Cook the pastry in an oven preheated to 180°C/Fan 160°C/Gas 4 for 15 minutes or until pale gold in colour.

Wrap each head of garlic in an individual piece of foil, adding a spoonful of oil to each package. Cook at 180°C/Fan 160°C/Gas 4 for 30 minutes.

When the garlic has cooled, squeeze each clove of garlic out of its skin and spread the resulting purée over the base of the pastry case.

Cook the bacon until crispy and sprinkle on top of the garlic purée.

Whisk the eggs into the cream, season and pour into the tart case.

Bake at 200°C/Fan 180°C/Gas 6 for 25 minutes.

Asparagus Tart

SERVES 4

This is the quickest, easiest tart ever; you don't even have to pre-cook the asparagus.

Cheese pastry
110g unsalted butter
140g plain flour
30g strong Cheddar
   or Parmesan, grated

Filling
1 bunch of asparagus,
   with the woody
   ends cut off
100g Parmesan,
   grated
200ml double cream
2 eggs, plus 2 extra
   yolks
salt and pepper

Put all the ingredients for the pastry into a food processor and mix until the dough forms a ball. Press the dough into a 20cm tart tin with a removable base. Prick really thoroughly all over, even up the sides (this will prevent shrinkage), then chill in the fridge.

Cook the pastry in an oven preheated to 180°C/Fan 160°C/Gas 4 for 15 minutes or until pale gold in colour.

Mix the cream, eggs and cheese in a bowl and season well.

Arrange the uncooked asparagus in the tart tin. I do it in a wheel shape, cutting the tops off so that the stems fit, and then sprinkling the tops amongst the 'spokes', but you can place the asparagus in rows if you prefer.

Pour over the cream mixture and bake the tart at 180°C/Fan 160°C/Gas 4 for about 40 minutes.

Mushroom Tart

SERVES 4

This takes a bit more time than most of the tarts I cook but it's delicious, and worth the effort in the autumn, when the mushrooms, whether shop bought or freshly picked, look so tempting.

Pastry
Use a 320g pack of the ready-rolled puff pastry you can buy in supermarkets, but make sure it's the kind with extra butter

Filling
10g dried mushrooms
50g unsalted butter
2 tbsp olive oil
1 large Spanish
    onion, thinly sliced
25g smoked bacon,
    cut into lardons
2 tbsp double cream
250g large field
    or Portobello
    mushrooms, cut
    into 1cm chunks
2 shallots,
    thinly sliced
1 sprig of thyme
25g Parmesan, shaved

Line a 20cm tart tin with the pastry, tucking in all the extra bits round the sides (this will make a better, stronger edging).

Cover the pastry with baking parchment, fill it with baking beans and cook for 20 minutes at 180°C/Fan 160°C/Gas 4. Remove the baking parchment and the beans and return the tart tin to the oven for another 5–10 minutes until the pastry has dried out and is golden.

Cover the dried mushrooms with boiling water and leave for 20 minutes. Drain, keeping the soaking water.

Heat half the butter and half the oil in a saucepan. Cook the onion and the bacon very gently, with the lid on, until the onion is completely soft. This will take at least 15 minutes.

Stir 3 tablespoons of the mushroom water into the onion and bacon mixture and then add the cream. Boil till it has reduced down by half and then whizz it all up in a food processor. You should have a thick purée.

Heat the remaining butter and oil and sauté the shallots. When they are soft, add the dried and the fresh mushrooms and cook for another 5 minutes.

Add the thyme, season and cook for another couple of minutes.

Spread the onion and bacon purée onto the tart case and warm it through. Top it with the warm mushroom mixture and scatter over the Parmesan shavings.

Tomato & Prosciutto Tart

SERVES 6

The starting point for this recipe was one by Tamasin Day-Lewis but my version — if it's possible — is even simpler. To me, it has every advantage: it's quick to make, redolent of summer, and the kitchen smells wonderful while it cooks. And everyone of every age seems to love eating it.

500g block of all-butter puff pastry (don't use ready rolled as it's not strong enough for this recipe)
10 slices jambon de Bayonne or Serrano ham (it's not worth using expensive Parma ham for this)
2 garlic cloves
1 tbsp chopped rosemary leaves
100ml olive oil
4 large tomatoes, sliced
a handful of basil leaves, torn
pepper

Roll the pastry out to about 30 x 18cm and put it on a baking tray lined with baking parchment.

Whizz up the ham, garlic, rosemary and some pepper with 50ml of olive oil until you have a rough paste.

Spread this mixture evenly over the pastry, leaving a margin of about 2cm all round. Then arrange the tomatoes on top, drizzle over the remaining oil and bake for 30 minutes at 200°C/Fan 180°C/Gas 6, or until the pastry is golden. Scatter over the torn basil leaves and then serve.

Two Tomato Tarts

The first tomato tart is summery and rather more sophisticated;
the second is homely and better for colder days.

TART ONE (SERVES 4)

Roll out some bought puff pastry to fit a 20cm tin. You can use ready-rolled for this and if it's a larger circle than your tin, fold the edges over on themselves to make a thicker rim.

Cover the pastry with a piece of baking parchment, fill it with baking beans and cook at 200°C/Fan 180°C/Gas 6 for 15 minutes.

Remove the parchment and beans and cook for another 5–10 minutes till the pastry has dried out and is golden. Then spread with 2 heaped tablespoons of sundried tomato paste.

Heat 3 tablespoons of olive oil in a frying pan and gently stew 225g of sliced red onions with 3 sliced garlic cloves, 1 teaspoon of white wine vinegar and 3 tablespoons of caster sugar for about 20 minutes until very soft.

Spread this mixture on top of the tomato paste and scatter over 20 chopped black olives and 50g of chopped anchovy fillets. Top with 10–12 halved cherry tomatoes and cook at 190°C/Fan 170°C/Gas 5 for 30 minutes.

TART TWO (SERVES 6)

Make some cheese pastry using 110g of butter, 140g of plain flour and 30g of grated strong Cheddar. Put all the ingredients into a food processor and mix until the dough forms a ball. Press the dough into a 23cm tart tin with a removable base – you will have only just enough. Prick really thoroughly all over, even up the sides (this will prevent shrinkage), then chill in the fridge.

Cook at 200°C/Fan 180°C/Gas 6 for 15 minutes or until golden. Brush the pastry with 2 tablespoons of sundried tomato paste.

Cut 8 plum tomatoes in half and arrange them in a roasting tin, cut side up. Sprinkle over 2 crushed cloves of garlic, a tablespoonful each of chopped rosemary and thyme, a pinch of chilli flakes, half a teaspoon of soft brown sugar, seasoning and 4 tablespoons of olive oil. Roast at 220°C/Fan 200°C/Gas 7 for 60 minutes.

Beat together 450g of crème fraîche with 2 whole eggs and an extra white and season well.

Arrange the tomatoes in the tart, cover with the egg mixture and scatter over 2 tablespoons of white breadcrumbs mixed with 1 tablespoon of grated Parmesan.

Cook at 220°C/Fan 200°C/Gas 7 for 40 minutes.

Cheese Roll

SERVES 6

Technically, this is not a tart, but it was constantly requested by the hordes of boys of every age who spent their summers at Le Rouzet. It is a quick, simple, cheap and filling lunch and 30 years on, we are still eating it. I serve it with a green salad dressed with walnut oil, a little lemon juice and a handful of toasted walnuts.

170g Philadelphia cheese (in France, I use St Môret)
115g Gruyère, grated
1 large garlic clove, crushed
500g block of all-butter puff pastry (ready-rolled puff pastry is too thin for this recipe)
1 egg yolk
salt and pepper

Nota Bene
An even quicker version is to simply wrap up a cheap Camembert in ready-rolled pastry, glaze with egg yolk and make an incision in the top. Cook it as you would the cheese roll.

Mix the cheeses and the garlic together. Season well.

Roll the pastry into a 20 x 30cm rectangle and spread the cheese mixture evenly all over it, leaving a margin of about 2.5cm all round.

Turn the edges over on themselves and roll up from the long side, gluing it together by brushing with the egg yolk.

Put the roll on to a tray lined with baking parchment, with the seam side down.

Make 3 short slashes in the top and glaze all over with the rest of the egg yolk.

Cook at 200°C/Fan 180°C/Gas 6 for about 40 minutes until the pastry is golden. If it browns too quickly, cover with foil and turn the oven down to 180°C/Fan 160°C/Gas 4.

To serve, cut both ends off (the pastry is a bit solid at the ends) and divide the rest into 6 portions – this is rich, so it goes a long way.

Cheese Soufflé Tart

SERVES 6

When in a real rush, I make a cheese soufflé mixture and bake it in cheese pastry. It's delicious but this is a much more interesting version and well worth the extra time and trouble.

Cheese pastry
110g butter
140g plain flour
30g Parmesan or
  strong Cheddar,
  grated
a pinch of paprika

Filling
3 eggs, separated
284ml double cream
2 level tsp Dijon
  mustard
150g Gruyère, grated
75g feta, crumbled
125g Brie, rind
  removed and
  cut into cubes
2 tbsp pine nuts
salt and pepper

Put all the ingredients for the pastry into a food processor and mix until the dough forms a ball. Press the dough into a 23cm loose-bottomed tart tin with a removable base (the pastry will be thin but that is what you want). Prick really thoroughly all over, even up the sides (this will prevent shrinkage), then chill in the fridge.

Cook the pastry in an oven preheated to 180°C/Fan 160°C/Gas 4 for 15 minutes or until pale gold in colour.

Whisk the egg yolks and cream together with the mustard and plenty of seasoning. Stir in the cheeses.

Whisk the egg whites until stiff and fold into the cheese and cream mixture. Pour into the pastry case. Sprinkle with pine nuts.

Bake at 180°C/Fan 160°C/Gas 4 for 40 minutes until set. Cool for 15 minutes before serving.

A tomato salad is a good accompaniment.

Prawn & Celeriac Tart

SERVES 6

A rich tart, this needs nothing more than a green salad with a mustardy dressing to accompany it. I often freeze tart cases with the ingredients already arranged in them, so that I have practically nothing left to do on the day, but I never freeze cooked tarts. There is nothing to beat one straight from the oven — and the kitchen smells wonderful.

Cheese pastry
110g butter
140g flour
30g strong Cheddar
 or Parmesan, grated

Filling
10 rashers of
 smoked streaky
 bacon, diced
180g celeriac,
 peeled and cut
 into small chunks
50g butter
18 large raw prawns,
 peeled and deveined
2 eggs, plus 2 extra
 yolks
300ml double cream
salt and pepper

Put all the ingredients for the pastry into a food processor and mix until the dough forms a ball. Press the dough into a 23cm loose-bottomed tart tin with a removable base (the pastry will be thin but that is what you want). Prick really thoroughly all over, even up the sides (this will prevent shrinkage), then chill in the fridge.

Cook the pastry in an oven preheated to 180°C/Fan 160°C/Gas 4 for 15 minutes or until pale gold in colour.

Sauté the bacon and celeriac in the butter until the celeriac is turning gold and the bacon is beginning to get crispy.

Arrange in the tart case with the raw prawns.

Whisk the eggs into the cream, season well and pour carefully into the tart case. Cook at 190°C/Fan 170°C/Gas 5 for 35–40 minutes.

DINNER
FIRST COURSES

Rounding up guests for meal times at Le Rouzet is like herding cats: there is always a child to be tucked up; the garden, littered with towels and toys, to be tidied; a last story to be told. It is, therefore, essential that the beginning of dinner can wait patiently until the last guest is ready and the candles are lit. And when that first course is finally produced it should be an enticement, as pretty as you can make it and a herald of things to come.

Avocado & Bacon Vinaigrette

SERVES 6

Year after year, our boys and their friends would ask for this. It was their favourite Le Rouzet first course and they would eat it as often as I was prepared to make it. The only difficulty I would have was finding enough ripe avocados in the local shops: the garden wall always had rows of them ripening in readiness, much prodded in anticipation by hungry boys. Nowadays, the recipe feels somewhat dated, but it's still good, hearty food in a rather reassuring way.

6 rashers of smoked streaky bacon
3 tomatoes, roughly chopped
3 tbsp red wine vinegar
75ml olive oil
2 tbsp Dijon mustard
3 ripe avocados
plenty of salt and pepper

Chop up the bacon and fry till crispy. Add the tomatoes, the vinegar and olive oil to the pan, stir in the mustard and bubble for one minute. Season generously.

Peel and halve the avocados and put a half on each plate. Pour over the bubbling dressing and serve immediately with lots of bread to mop up the juices.

Two Ways with Asparagus

SERVES 4

When asparagus begins to get cheaper and you want an alternative to serving it with butter, here are two useful recipes.

a large handful
of parsley
a small handful
of mint
a small handful
of basil
1 dessertspoon capers
1 dessertspoon
Dijon mustard
100ml olive oil
450g asparagus,
cooked till
just tender
6 rashers of streaky
bacon, cut into
lardons and
fried until crisp
Parmesan shavings
or wafers (optional)
salt and pepper

WITH SAUCE VERTE AND BACON

Put all the herbs, the capers and mustard into a food processor and grind to a paste. Add the olive oil slowly till you get the consistency you want. Season the sauce well.

To serve, put the asparagus on to a large plate and scatter over the crispy bacon and the Parmesan shavings or wafers. Serve the sauce separately.

Nota Bene
It's incredibly quick and easy to make Parmesan wafers and they look pretty and professional. Grate some Parmesan coarsely – a tablespoon makes one wafer – and arrange in circles, about 8cm in diameter, on a baking tray lined with baking parchment. Cook for 5–8 minutes at 200°C/Fan 180°C/Gas 6, taking them out as soon as they are golden.

Leave the wafers for a minute or so before easing them off the baking parchment: you are releasing them rather than moving them. Don't pile them up on a plate, as they may well stick to one another). These have to be made the day you are eating them or they will go soggy.

1 slice of strong
  white bread
  without crusts
60ml olive oil
1 tsp sherry vinegar
100g ground almonds
25g mint leaves
450g asparagus,
  cooked till
  just tender
a few blanched
  almonds, toasted,
  for decoration
1 garlic clove, crushed
salt and pepper

WITH ALMOND AND MINT SAUCE

Soak the bread in 150ml of cold water.

In a food processor, whizz up the bread
(reserve the soaking water), the oil, vinegar,
ground almonds and almost all the mint until
you have a smooth sauce. Add enough of the
soaking water to give you the consistency
you want. Season.

Divide the asparagus between the plates
and decorate with the toasted almonds and
a few mint leaves. Serve the sauce separately.

Asparagus Frittatas

SERVES 6

*These make a good, rather than a spectacular, first course,
but they have a great advantage – apart from the final cooking,
the mixture can be made well in advance and you can vary
the ingredients, depending on what you have to hand.
They freeze well and can be reheated gently.*

I large onion,
finely diced
1 tbsp olive oil
6 rashers of back
bacon or slices
of cheap Parma
ham, diced
200g asparagus,
stems chopped
7 eggs
350ml double cream
1 tbsp finely chopped
parsley
100g Gruyère, grated
a handful of
salad leaves
salt and pepper

Lightly oil 6 ramekin dishes.

Gently fry the onion in olive oil until it is
very soft. Then add the bacon or Parma ham
and continue to fry until cooked. Stir in the
(uncooked) asparagus and divide between
the ramekins.

Mix together the eggs, cream, parsley,
Gruyère and seasoning and pour over
the asparagus.

Cook the frittatas at 180°C/Fan 160°C/
Gas 4 for 25 minutes till they are puffy but firm.
Turn out on to individual plates and decorate
with a few salad leaves.

It is really isn't essential to turn these
little frittatas out – I only do it for the sake
of elegance. You can serve them as they
are in their ramekin dishes.

Avocado, Pomegranate & Pine Nuts

SERVES 6

This is really a construction of delicious ingredients, since there is very little cooking involved. I use individual ring moulds to make sure that these are all the same size and height – it would be tricky to make this dish without them – and I always buy an extra avocado to be on the safe side.

4 large avocados
lemon juice
a handful of rocket or
  mâche, leaves torn
8 rashers of smoked
  streaky bacon,
  cooked till crispy,
  then crumbled
seeds of 1
  pomegranate
3 tbsp toasted
  pine nuts
a mustardy
  vinaigrette

Peel and halve the avocados, then slice them widthways so that you have a selection of half moon shapes. Brush them with lemon juice and use them to line each ring mould. You want to build up a wall of avocado round the edges, leaving the centre empty.

Fill the centre of each ring with the salad leaves and top this with the bacon, followed by the pomegranate seeds and the pine nuts.

Leave this mixture in the rings until you are ready to serve and then drizzle over some mustardy vinaigrette. Carefully unmould each ring and serve.

Grilled Vegetables
with Walnut Sauce

SERVES 6

*Our garden is full of walnut trees, but generally the red squirrels win
the race to collect the nuts. However, over the years, I have collected
recipes using walnuts in the hope that one day there will be enough
nuts for all of us. Here is one of my favourite uses for them and
it is equally good as a lunchtime salad.*

4 courgettes,
1 aubergine
olive oil
3 Romano peppers
(if you can't get
them, ordinary
ones will do
but will need
longer cooking)

Walnut sauce
1 thick slice of good
white bread
2 large garlic cloves
100g walnuts
100ml olive oil
juice of ½ lemon
150ml natural
yoghurt
2 tbsp dill
salt and pepper

Slice the courgettes lengthways and the
aubergine into thick slices. Brush them with
oil and griddle until they are soft, in batches
if necessary.

Drizzle the peppers with a little olive oil
and cook at 200°C/Fan 180°C/Gas 6 for
15 minutes. Arrange all the vegetables on
a serving dish.

For the walnut sauce, put the bread, garlic,
walnuts, olive oil, lemon juice, yoghurt and
dill into a food processor with 50ml of water.
Season generously and whizz up together.

Serve the sauce in a pretty bowl, along
with the grilled vegetables.

Broad Bean & Pea Salad

SERVES 6

If you are using broad beans, either fresh or frozen, it is really important to peel off their coats. Cover them in boiling water for a few minutes and they will come off very easily. The effort is worth it, as the beans look beautiful and taste delicious. However, if you are short of time, use soya beans. I don't bother to cook either kind of bean, nor indeed the peas.

250g fresh or frozen broad beans, skins removed
150g frozen peas
a handful of mint leaves
zest of 2 lemons
1 garlic clove, crushed
olive oil
250g good mozzarella or – even better – burrata
6 slices of Parma ham (the cheapest you can find) or pancetta
50g shelled pistachios, toasted and chopped
salt and pepper

Mix the beans and peas together and, if frozen, leave them to defrost.

Pat them dry and mix with the mint and lemon zest, garlic, some olive oil and seasoning.

Arrange on a serving plate with the torn mozzarella or the burrata.

Cook the Parma ham in a hot oven until it is very crispy. Then crumble it up and scatter it and the pistachios all over the top of the salad.

Nota Bene
I hate throwing anything away and one day, confronted by a whole bowlful of broad bean skins and with time to spare, I decided to see if I could transform them into something edible. Throw a handful or so of flour into the bowl of bean skins and mix it all up with a little water. Deep fry the bean skins in small batches in sunflower oil until they are brown and crispy and then sprinkle them with salt and a bit of chilli powder. Rather to my surprise they are very good with a glass of wine before supper, and although they are rather time consuming, they can be made hours in advance.

Marinated Figs
with Camembert

SERVES 4

*This salad is particularly good when the walnuts on our trees
at Le Rouzet are just ripe – 'wet' – but it is still excellent if
you use ordinary dry walnuts, as long as you toast them first.
Whenever you toast any nuts, rub off the skins between your
hands when they have cooled down. For the marinade,
any cheap supermarket balsamic vinegar is perfect.*

200ml balsamic
  vinegar
100g caster sugar
2 garlic cloves
6 thyme sprigs
6 ripe figs, halved
a bag of watercress
  or rocket
150g ripe Camembert
  or similar soft
  cheese, the runnier
  the better
4 tbsp walnut oil
75g walnuts
salt and pepper

Put the vinegar, sugar, garlic and thyme in a
pan and boil to dissolve the sugar. Remove from
the heat and pour the marinade over the figs.
Leave for a couple of hours.

Heat a frying pan, drain the figs and sear
them, cut side down, till they caramelise.
You may have to add a small amount of
the marinade to stop them sticking.

Arrange the watercress, the figs and the
cheese on plates, season and drizzle with
the walnut oil. Scatter the nuts on top.

Celeriac Remoulade
& Prawns

SERVES 6

*A beautiful first course, and no trouble to anyone. I have been making
this since my father came up with the original idea in the 1970s.
Indeed, I made it for the dinner party he organised after our wedding
because it was the simplest thing I could think of (the custom in those
days was for the bridal couple to leave after the speeches, but my
father, quite rightly, wanted the party to continue).*

1 celeriac, peeled
and shredded
4–5 tbsp
crème fraîche
1 tbsp Dijon mustard
200g large prawns,
cooked, shelled
and deveined
olive oil and sherry
vinegar
3 large handfuls
of rocket
salt and pepper

Mix the celeriac into the crème fraîche
together with the mustard and season
with salt and pepper. Arrange it in a circle
on a large plate. The celeriac needs to be
really rich and creamy, so you may have
to add a bit more crème fraîche.

Dress the prawns with a small amount of
olive oil and sherry vinegar. Fill the centre
of the celeriac with rocket and pile the
prawns on top.

Prawn & Bacon Salad

SERVES 6

*To me, this is an ideal summery first course, served with good bread
to mop up any juices, but it works just as well as a lunch dish,
in which case these quantities would serve three.*

1 small garlic
  clove, crushed
juice and zest
  of 1 lemon
a pinch of dried
  chillies
a small bunch
  of chives
6 tbsp strong olive oil
2 tsp soy sauce
18 large cooked and
  shelled prawns
85g streaky bacon,
  cut into strips
100g bag of mixed
  salad leaves
salt and pepper

Mix the garlic, lemon juice and zest, chillies, chives, 2 tablespoons of the olive oil and the soy sauce in a bowl. Add the prawns and leave in the fridge for an hour.

Heat a tablespoon of olive oil and cook the bacon until crispy.

Tip in the prawns and their marinade and stir till they are piping hot – a couple of minutes.

Toss the salad leaves with the remaining oil and spoon the prawns over the leaves. You may need just a bit of extra lemon juice on the leaves.

Marinated Prawns

SERVES 4

This is a horribly messy first course but it's delicious and needs to be prepared in advance, which to me is always an advantage.

a walnut-sized knob of root ginger, peeled
4 small red chillies, deseeded
2 fat garlic cloves peeled
2 tsp cumin seeds
1 tbsp garam masala
2 tsp turmeric
3 tbsp lemon juice
200g Greek yoghurt
20 really large prawns
2 limes, to serve
salt and pepper

Whizz up the ginger, chillies, garlic, cumin seeds, garam masala, turmeric and lemon juice with 2 tablespoons of water in a food processor until you have a smooth sauce. Add the yoghurt, season and mix well. Stir in the prawns and leave overnight, covered, in the fridge.

Remove the prawns from the fridge so they are at room temperature before you cook them. Either griddle or barbecue them for 3–4 minutes until they are golden.

Serve at once with the lime halves and lots of napkins.

Smoked Haddock Mousse

SERVES 8

These are absolutely no trouble but when decorated with a bit of watercress, they look pretty enough for a dinner party and you can put them ready them hours in advance. Serve warm.

225g smoked haddock, skinned and roughly chopped
a pinch of cayenne pepper
⅓ tsp freshly grated nutmeg
2 eggs, lightly beaten
275ml double cream
1 dessertspoon chopped chives
300g sliced smoked salmon
watercress
salt

Whizz up the smoked haddock in a food processor, add the cayenne pepper and nutmeg and season with salt to taste.

Add the eggs and mix again. Finally whizz in the cream and chives.

Line 8 ramekins with the slices of smoked salmon. As long as the bottoms of the dishes are covered with a complete slice (so that the mixture can't seep out) it doesn't matter if you use up bits and pieces of the smoked salmon around the sides.

Fill each ramekin three-quarters full with the smoked haddock mixture. Put the ramekins in a roasting tin and add enough boiling water to come halfway up their sides. Cook for exactly 30 minutes at 190°C/Fan 170° C/Gas 5.

Loosen the sides of the mousses and turn out on to individual plates. I do this by covering each ramekin with a clean tea towel and shaking the mousse into the cloth in my hand so that it ends up on the plate the right way up. Decorate with watercress.

Watercress & Smoked Salmon 'Tarts'

MAKES 12

These are a light and quick version of a tart: instead of pastry, you use smoked salmon or Parma ham – both are equally good. They will sit happily in the fridge for hours until you are ready to cook them.

250g smoked salmon or Parma ham. If you are using Parma ham, trim off the fat around the edges.
4 eggs
120ml double cream
zest of ½ lemon
120g watercress, finely chopped
1 heaped tbsp capers, rinsed and chopped
salt and pepper

Butter 6 ramekins dishes and line each one with smoked salmon or Parma ham. Trim the edges and use the snippings to fill any gaps.

Whisk the eggs and cream together and then stir in the lemon zest, watercress, capers, a bit of salt and lots of black pepper.

Spoon the mixture into the 'tart' cases and bake for 20 minutes until just firm at 200°C/Fan 180°C/Gas 6.

Remove the 'tarts' from the oven and leave them to stand for a few minutes before running a knife round the edges. Then cover your hand with a tea towel, unmould them upside down into your palm and serve the right way up.

Smoked Salmon
& Avocado Tarts

SERVES 8

I make these in individual tart tins, each about 8cm in diameter, which turns this into an elegant first course but one that can mostly be done well ahead of time. If you are in a rush, use the celeriac remoulade you can buy in any French supermarket, but add the horseradish and herbs.

Cheese pastry
110g butter
140g plain flour
30g strong Cheddar
  or Parmesan,
  grated

Salad
1 small celeriac,
  peeled and
  shredded
1 tbsp lemon juice
3 tbsp crème fraîche
3 tsp creamed
  horseradish
2 tbsp chopped chives
1 tbsp chopped
  tarragon leaves
salt and pepper

Filling
3 ripe avocados
1 tbsp lemon juice
400g smoked salmon,
  cut into strips
salt and pepper

Put all the ingredients for the pastry into a food processor and mix until the dough forms a ball. Line the tart cases with the pastry, prick very thoroughly all over and chill well. Any leftover pastry freezes beautifully.

Cook the little tarts in an oven preheated to 180°C/Fan 160°C/Gas 4 for about 15 minutes or until golden. If they look as if they are bubbling up a bit during the cooking, press the pastry down hard using kitchen paper and return to the oven.

Mix the celeriac with the lemon juice, crème fraîche, horseradish and herbs and season well.

When you are ready to eat, preheat the oven to 180°C/Fan 160°C/Gas 4. Peel and slice the avocados and toss with the lemon juice. Add the smoked salmon strips and divide between the little tart cases. Cook for 10 minutes – all you are really doing is warming them through – and serve them with a spoonful of the celeriac.

Smoked Salmon
& Chive Creams

SERVES 6

Long ago, we ate something similar to this at Le Gavroche and here is my rather homespun and certainly very easy version. It makes a good first course for a dinner party and, apart from the final cooking, can all be done in advance.

400ml double cream
60g chives, chopped
300g smoked
   salmon, snipped
6 soft-boiled
   quails' eggs
salt and pepper

Put the cream and the chives in a small pan, bring to the boil and simmer very gently for 5 minutes. Tip the mixture into a food processor and whizz it up for 2–3 minutes. It is important to do it for this long: the cream will turn a wonderful pea green colour and you won't need to sieve the mixture.

Mix the fish into the cream and season with lots of pepper and just a tiny bit of salt.

Divide the mixture between 4 ramekins and put them into a roasting tin. Add enough boiling water to come halfway up their sides and cook for 8 minutes or until firm to the touch at 180°C/Fan 160°C/Gas 4.

Serve with a quails' egg on top of each ramekin and perhaps some Melba toast.

Nota Bene
To cook the quails' eggs, put them into a pan of cold water, bring to the boil, then take the pan off the heat and leave for 30 seconds before draining. Remove the shells when cold.

Scallops & Chorizo

SERVES 4

I pulled this recipe out of a magazine years ago and have been cooking it ever since. It's not ideal for a large number of guests, as you have to fry the scallops at the last moment, but for a few people, it's a delicious treat.

1 preserved lemon
2 tbsp chopped parsley
1 large garlic clove, crushed
a good squeeze of fresh lemon juice
250g chorizo. sliced into 2cm rings
8–12 fat scallops
clarified butter, ghee or 1 tbsp olive oil
a handful of rocket
salt and pepper

Cut the rind off the lemon and slice it as thinly as you can. Add it to the parsley and garlic with a good squeeze of fresh lemon juice, season and set aside.

Cook the chorizo in its own fat until it is golden, then keep it warm.

Heat the butter, ghee or oil until really hot. (I use ghee because it seems to caramelise the scallops better than anything else.)

Cook the scallops, without moving them, for a minute on either side. Then arrange some salad leaves on each plate, spoon over the scallops and pan juices, add the chorizo and sprinkle over the preserved lemon mixture. Serve immediately.

A Connaught Grill Classic

SERVES 4

My father specialised in spoiling me and when I was about to give birth to our eldest son, John, he sent me a huge cheque with strict instructions to spend it entirely on treats. He suggested that one of those treats should be dinner at the Connaught, a place we both loved and where he had given me a wonderfully indulgent 21ˢᵗ birthday party. We had a superb dinner but it was the first course that was most memorable and this is my attempt to recreate it. Although it is a bit time consuming and really shouldn't be included in a book dedicated to speed, each stage is very simple and it can all be done hours ahead.

Cheese pastry
110g plain flour
140g butter
30g strong Cheddar, grated

Filling
4 quails' eggs
juice of 1 lemon
100g butter, cut into small chunks
1 jar of L'Aquila Salsa Truffina (available online; an essential in my store cupboard)
3 egg yolks
salt and pepper

Put all the ingredients for the pastry into a food processor and mix until the dough forms a ball. Press the dough into individual tart cases, each one 8cm in diameter. Prick very thoroughly all over, even up the sides, and chill.

Bake at 180°C/Fan 160°C/Gas 4 for about 15 minutes until golden. You will have a great deal of leftover pastry but it freezes extremely well.

Soft boil the quails' eggs by putting them in a pan of cold water, bringing them to the boil and cooking them for 30 seconds. Drain them in cold water and tap them to stop them cooking. Peel them when they are quite cold.

Using the same pan, bring the lemon juice to the boil and reduce by half. Then take the pan off the heat and whisk the egg yolks into the lemon juice.

Return the pan to the very lowest heat possible and add a couple of chunks of butter, stirring all the time. If you think the mixture is getting too hot, take the pan off the heat for a moment or two but continue to whisk. When the first chunks of butter have melted, add the next couple and continue stirring until you have a thick sauce. The end result should be a rather thicker than normal Hollandaise sauce.

When the sauce is thick enough, season it well and pour it into a thermos flask. It will keep for hours like this – I frequently make it in the late afternoon for dinner.

Carefully unmould the tart cases and decant the mushroom mixture (the L'Aquila Salsa) into a heatproof bowl. Place both on a baking tray in a low oven to warm everything through.

When you are ready to serve, divide the mushroom mixture between the tart cases, top with a quails' egg, then dollop a good amount of the sauce on top.

Nota Bene
Salsa Truffina, made by L'Aquila and available on line, is a paste made of mushrooms and black truffles. It is delicious and try as I might I can never make anything to match it. Spread it on toast and top it with buttered eggs, add cream to turn it into a sauce for pasta, stuff a pork fillet with it before you wrap everything up in Parma ham or pastry – these are just a few reasons why I always have a supply of it. The jars have a long shelf life, so it's worth buying several at a time.

DINNER
VEGETABLES

I find that vegetables needing last-minute attention are very distracting: all that timing and straining takes one away from one's guests and creates an unnecessary commotion in the kitchen. The recipes in this chapter are suitable for large numbers, can be done in advance and reheated, and a good many of them can be frozen; in other words, they are very forgiving and will wait patiently until you are ready for them.

Carrot Purée

SERVES 4

Carrot purée is beautiful, can take the place of gravy and freezes well.

2 shallots, peeled
and finely sliced
50g butter
500g carrots, peeled
and chopped
284ml double cream
salt and pepper

Sweat the shallots in the butter gently for 10 minutes or until soft. Then add the carrots, a tablespoon of water and a pinch of salt. Cover and cook very gently until the carrots are tender. Add the cream, turn up the heat and bubble briskly for about 3 minutes to reduce the cream.

Tip the contents of the pan into a food processor and whizz till you have a smooth purée. Season well. If the carrots are a bit bland, add a pinch of caster sugar.

This can be reheated and kept in a warming oven.

Carrots in Crème Fraîche

SERVES 4

This is an incredibly useful recipe in that it can be made hours ahead and reheated. Also, since the carrots are cooked in what amounts to a sauce, you don't need gravy if serving them with plain meat. Cauliflower florets work just as well.

4 good-sized carrots, peeled and cut into rounds
a knob of butter
8 rashers of smoked streaky bacon, chopped
8 heaped tbsp crème fraîche
salt and pepper

Cook the carrots until they are al dente, then plunge them into cold water so that they stop cooking.

Melt the butter in the same pan in which you have cooked the carrots and fry the bacon until it is becoming crispy. Then ladle in the crème fraîche, scraping up all the brown bits in the pan, add the carrots and season well. You can leave them like this until you need them. When you reheat them, the crème fraîche will turn into a thick sauce.

Tomatoes with Mozzarella & Breadcrumbs

SERVES 6

*There is nothing particularly exciting about this but, as it requires
no last-minute attention, it's a very useful recipe to serve with plain
barbecued meat. Also, it will wait patiently in the oven.*

6 good-sized tomatoes
180g fresh white
 breadcrumbs
8 anchovy fillets,
 chopped
2 large garlic
 cloves, crushed
a handful of parsley,
 chopped
1 ball of mozzarella,
 finely diced
6 tbsp olive oil
salt and pepper

Slice the tomatoes in half, scoop out the seeds
and mix these scoopings with the breadcrumbs,
anchovies, garlic, parsley, diced mozzarella
and 2 tablespoons of the oil. Season with
salt and pepper.

Pile the mixture into the tomato halves,
pour over the rest of the oil and cook at
200°C/Fan 180°C/Gas 6 for 25 minutes.

Stuffed Mushrooms

SERVES 4

'Life's too short to stuff a mushroom' but, since you can rustle these up in no time at all, I take issue with Shirley Conran's famous quote. When we were first married, I used to make these as a first course; nowadays I serve them with plain barbecued meat. They may be dated, but they are too good to jettison simply because of fashion (or clever quips). Unlike so many vegetable dishes, they are extremely forgiving: they can be frozen (cooked or uncooked) and will sit for ages in the oven without coming to any harm.

4 large mushrooms
15g butter
4 rashers of streaky
  bacon, chopped
20g fresh white
  breadcrumbs
2 tsp finely chopped
  parsley
60g Cheddar, grated
juice and grated zest
  of ½ lemon
salt and pepper

Remove the stalks from the mushrooms, chop them roughly and fry them in the butter together with the bacon.

Stir in the breadcrumbs, parsley, cheese, lemon juice and zest, then season well. Pile this mixture firmly on top of the mushrooms and cook at 150°C/Fan 130°C/Gas 2 for 20 minutes.

Bean & Herb Purée

SERVES 3

Another vegetable recipe that can be reheated, this uses those wonderful tins of flageolet beans that you find in any French supermarket and which are so much better than their English counterparts. In England, I use haricot or cannellini beans and coriander. In France, I substitute them with flageolet beans and parsley since coriander is impossible to find – both versions are excellent.

1 onion, thinly sliced
50g butter
4 large garlic cloves, crushed
400g tin of flageolet or haricot beans
a small handful of parsley or coriander
2 tbsp olive oil
salt and pepper

Cook the onion slowly in the butter until it's very soft, adding the garlic to the pan for the final 5 minutes. Then whizz this mixture in a food processor with the beans, herbs and olive oil and season with salt and pepper. Tip it all into the pan to warm through.

If you are making this in advance and reheating it, do so very gently; you may need to add a tablespoonful of water to help the purée regain its consistency.

Broccoli, Chilli & Flaked Almonds

SERVES 4

Because this is a dish that can be reheated, it's very useful and I have found that cauliflower works just as well as broccoli. I put quite a lot of chilli in the recipe but if that doesn't appeal, halve the amount and the result will still be excellent.

1 large head of
broccoli or a
small cauliflower
3 tbsp olive oil
2 tbsp cumin seeds
2 garlic cloves,
crushed
2 red chillies,
finely sliced
150g flaked almonds
2 tbsp chopped
parsley
salt and pepper

Fry the broccoli or cauliflower in the olive oil until the edges are dark gold, then reduce the heat, cover and cook for a couple of minutes. You want it still to retain some bite.

Add the cumin, garlic, chillies and almonds and continue to fry, uncovered, for another 5 minutes. Season generously and stir in the chopped parsley.

If you are making this in advance, follow the recipe right up until the final 5 minutes of frying, then do that at the last minute.

Two Favourite
Brussels Sprout Recipes

500g Brussels sprouts
2 tbsp olive oil
salt

ROASTED BRUSSELS SPROUTS (SERVES 4)
*I love these just as they are but you could make
them more interesting by adding lardons or
chestnuts to the roasting tin.*

Trim and halve the Brussels sprouts and
put them in a roasting tin with the oil and
a generous amount of salt. Roast at 220°C/
Fan 200°C/Gas 7 for 15 minutes.

500g Brussels sprouts
50g butter
6 tbsp double cream
salt, pepper
    and nutmeg

PURÉED BRUSSELS SPROUTS (SERVES 4)
*This purée is curiously difficult to identify,
so you may be able to serve it to sprout haters.
It's wonderfully rich and can be reheated,
but it does need a lot of seasoning.*

Trim and cook the Brussels sprouts till tender.
Drain and whizz them up in a food processor
with the butter, cream, salt, pepper and lots
of nutmeg.

Courgette Ribbons

SERVES 6

*My favourite way of cooking courgettes, this not only looks pretty
but is also very forgiving. You can cook the courgettes almost to
the point of serving hours in advance, then reheat them quickly,
tossing them over a high heat.*

6 courgettes
50ml olive oil
3 garlic cloves,
    crushed
salt and pepper

Using a potato peeler, shave the courgettes
into strips and toss them with the oil and the
garlic over a medium heat. You need to keep
moving them, but it will only take a minute
or so for them to begin to wilt.

If you are not serving the courgettes at once,
turn off the heat at this point; they will sit
perfectly happily for hours and respond well
to a quick heat through. Season them well.

Cauliflower & Potatoes

SERVES 6

This recipe is based on Madhur Jaffrey's version of an Indian classic and I include it here because it's a great family favourite. You can do it all in advance and it will stand on its own as a simple lunch, as well as being delicious with any barbecued meat.

450g potatoes
6 tbsp vegetable oil
1 tsp cumin seeds
450g cauliflower
 florets
1 tsp ground cumin
1 tsp coriander seeds
½ tsp ground
 coriander
½ tsp turmeric
½ tsp cayenne
1 chilli, deseeded
 and chopped
1 tsp salt
pepper

Boil the potatoes – you don't need to peel them at this stage – and allow them to cool completely. When they are cold, peel them and chop into 3cm chunks.

Heat the oil in a large frying pan and roast the cumin seeds for a few seconds. Add the cauliflower, brown it more or less all over and then cover the pan and cook it for about 5 minutes until it's done but still firm.

Add the potatoes, the ground cumin, both kinds of coriander, turmeric, cayenne, chilli, salt and some pepper and mix well.

You can prepare the recipe up to this point hours in advance and reheat it, uncovered, until everything is piping hot. Or you can serve it straight away.

Potatoes in Mushroom Stock

SERVES 4

I rely on vegetable dishes that don't take me away from our guests and can be reheated quickly and easily. This recipe uses mushroom stock cubes called Star Porcini Mushroom and which are simply delicious. They are an essential part of my store cupboard and can be bought online.

4 medium-sized potatoes, sliced thickly (any variety of potato works for this recipe)
2 tbsp duck fat
600ml of mushroom stock, made with 30g dried mushrooms or 2 Star stock cubes
2 garlic cloves, crushed
a bunch of parsley, chopped
pepper

If making stock with dried mushrooms, soak them in 600ml of boiling water for 20 minutes. Strain off the liquid and chop the mushrooms very finely.

Sauté the potatoes in the duck fat until they are brown all over, then remove from the pan and set aside.

Tip in the stock, add the garlic and the parsley (and the dried mushrooms if you have them) and bubble for a minute or two to cook the garlic and to get the strength of the stock right – it might need reducing a little.

Then add the sautéed potatoes, season with lots of pepper (the stock cubes will give you all the salt you need) and reheat.

Flageolet Beans
& Tomatoes

SERVES 6

This is another way of using the tins of flageolet beans
you find in France and it goes wonderfully with lamb.
In England, haricot beans are a good alternative.
This recipe can be reheated and frozen.

150g shallots,
  finely sliced
100g butter
3 garlic cloves,
  crushed
100ml white wine
200ml chicken stock
  (a stock cube is fine)
4 tomatoes, deseeded
800g tin of flageolet
  beans, drained
4 tbsp chopped
  parsley
salt and pepper

Cook the shallots in the butter very slowly until they are completely soft, adding the garlic for the last few minutes. Add the wine and stock, bring it to the boil and tip in the tomatoes and the beans.

Bubble everything up for a couple of minutes to reduce it slightly and cook the tomatoes, then add the parsley and seasoning.

Haricots Blancs

SERVES 6

In France, I always have a good supply of tinned beans and lentils. They are invaluable when the house is full, as it takes no time to transform them into something delicious and, unlike fresh vegetables, they can be heated up and even frozen.

400g tin of haricot or cannellini beans, drained
250ml double cream
2 tsp Dijon mustard
2 tbsp chopped chives
2 tsp chopped tarragon leaves
salt and pepper

Tip the beans into a saucepan and add the other ingredients. Season really well and let the cream bubble up for a couple of minutes until it thickens a little. This can be reheated and is particularly good with pork.

Roasted Root Vegetables

SERVES 6

Use any combination of root vegetables you like; the semolina
makes them particularly crispy.

2kg assorted root
  vegetables
5 tbsp semolina
60g Parmesan, grated
2 tbsp chopped
  rosemary
olive oil
salt and pepper

Peel the vegetables and cut them into chunks of about the same size. In a bowl, mix the semolina, Parmesan and rosemary and season well with salt and pepper.

Pour some olive oil into a roasting tin to a depth of about 5mm and heat. When it's hot, add the vegetables and the semolina, Parmesan and rosemary and mix until everything is evenly coated.

Cook at 190°C/Fan 170°C/Gas 5 for about 45 minutes or until the vegetables are crispy.

DINNER
MAIN COURSES

The barbecue is a very important part of Le Rouzet life, but I have learnt that I can't trespass too much on the kindness and willingness of my sous chefs. For that reason, I have acquired a number of very simple, very quick recipes that don't take me away from our guests for too long: I don't really want anyone to notice that I am in the kitchen at all. While these recipes suit life in the French countryside perfectly, they are sophisticated enough for any dinner party back home.

Duck & Lentils

SERVES 6

This is staple food in Southwest France, where the cookery revolves around duck. I use tinned lentils, not only because it cuts down on the time involved in cooking this (very simple) dish, but also because they are extremely good.

½ duck breast per person
150g butter
3 large onions, thinly sliced
2 packets of smoked lardons
1 large tin of Lentilles Préparées or 350g Puy lentils (see below)
1 dessertspoon tomato purée
1 chicken stock cube
200ml red wine
salt and pepper

Nota Bene
When in France, buy an 800g tin of Lentilles Préparées. Failing that, cook 350g Puy lentils with a bay leaf for 25–30 minutes.
Liquid stock is sold in all French supermarkets and is an essential for every store cupboard.

The duck is best cooked on a barbecue but if you don't have one, score the skins and sear the fatty side of the breasts until golden brown in a dry frying pan. Turn the duck over and seal the other side. Transfer to a baking dish and cook for 12 minutes at 200°C/Fan 180°C/Gas 6.

To make the lentils, melt the butter and very slowly, with the lid on the pan, cook the onions and the bacon. It will take about 30 minutes and by that time the onions will be very soft and translucent.

Tip in the lentils, add the tomato purée, stock cube, red wine and lots of seasoning.

Bring to the boil and cook briskly for about 5 minutes until the flavours all come together and the liquid has reduced a little. Season well. You are looking for a rich, earthy taste, so you might need to add a dash of balsamic vinegar or some liquid stock.

The lentils can be prepared a day ahead or even frozen.

Slice the duck thinly and arrange on each plate on top of a mound of lentils.

Pheasant or Duck Salad

SERVES 4

Whenever I am lucky enough to be given some pheasant I make this recipe. Avoid using chicken breasts, as they don't give the same depth of flavour. In France, with no pheasant, I use duck aiguilettes, which are thin slices of duck taken from between the breast and the carcass. They are cheaper (and have a rather more subtle taste) than a magret.

4 pheasant breasts,
  or 16 aiguillettes
  or 2 duck magrets
1 tbsp grated fresh
  root ginger
1 tbsp honey
1 garlic clove, crushed
1 tsp thyme leaves
3 tbsp olive oil

Dressing
4 tbsp walnut oil
1 tbsp olive oil
zest and juice
  of 1 orange
½ tbsp honey
salt and pepper

Salad
100g pancetta
2 tbsp pistachios,
  toasted and
  roughly chopped
3 heads of chicory

Cut whichever meat you are using into bite-sized bits and marinate in the ginger, honey, garlic, thyme, salt and pepper for as long as you have got, but for at least an hour. To get ahead, I usually do this part the day before.

Whisk together all the ingredients for the dressing and season.

Dry fry the pancetta till crisp and roughly break it up.

Heat the oil in a large frying pan and pour the meat and the marinade into the hot oil. Cook for about 5 minutes until the meat is brown and sticky.

Arrange the chicory leaves on a large plate in a circle and put the meat in the middle. Scatter over the pancetta and pistachios and pour over the dressing. Serve at once.

Oriental Duck Salad

SERVES 4

A quick salad ideal for a hot evening.

2 duck breasts
a large bag
of interesting
salad leaves

Dressing
4 tbsp fish sauce
juice of 1 lime
juice of 1 orange
2 red chillies,
  deseeded and
  finely chopped
2.5cm piece of fresh
  root ginger, grated
2–3 tbsp sesame oil

Mix together the fish sauce, the juice of the lime and the orange, the chillies and ginger. Add the sesame oil to taste.

The duck is best cooked on a barbecue but if you don't have one, score the skin and sear the breasts in a hot frying pan until the skin is golden brown. Turn them over and sear the other side briefly.

Roast at 220°C/Fan 200°C/Gas 7 for 12 minutes. When the duck has rested, slice it thinly – it should be pink in the middle – and serve warm or at room temperature.

Arrange on a plate on top of the salad leaves and pour over the dressing.

Duck Legs with Chorizo

SERVES 4

Confit of duck is on sale in every shop and market throughout Southwest France and it is so good that it really isn't worth making your own. If you can't find it, use ordinary duck legs and no one, other than you, will be able to tell the difference. If you are using confit, just scrape the excess fat off each leg and continue with the recipe.

4 confit or uncooked duck legs, rubbed with salt
800g salad potatoes
200g chorizo, the strong kind, chopped into chunks
4 garlic cloves, thinly sliced
1 red pepper, deseeded and chopped
3 tbsp red wine vinegar
4 large sprigs of rosemary, leaves only, chopped
salt and cayenne pepper

Put the duck legs on a rack over a roasting tin and cook at 200°C/Fan 180°C/Gas 6 for an hour till the skin is very crispy.

Cut the potatoes into 2cm chunks and simmer until just soft. Drain and put to one side.

Cook the chunks of chorizo gently in a dry frying pan until they have produced lots of oil. Take them out and then cook the potatoes and the pepper in the chorizo oil. There should be enough oil to turn the potatoes golden but if not, add either a tablespoonful or two of olive oil or some of the fat you have scraped off the duck legs when you took them out of their confit.

When all the potatoes are golden and crunchy, add the vinegar and reduce it by three quarters to make a glaze.

Tip in the chorizo and the rosemary, season with salt and cayenne pepper and serve with the duck legs.

Chicken & Mango Salad

SERVES 4

This is an ideal main course on a hot summer's evening.

3 boneless, skinless
  chicken breasts
3 tbsp sunflower oil
8 spring onions,
  finely sliced
8 garlic cloves,
  thinly sliced
2 unripe mangoes
1 Granny Smith apple
3 red chillies,
  deseeded and
  finely sliced
a bunch of coriander,
  roughly chopped
a bunch of mint,
  roughly chopped
rocket or watercress
3 tbsp roughly
  chopped roasted
  peanuts

Dressing
2 tbsp fish sauce
1½ tbsp caster sugar
zest and juice
  of 2 limes
2 tbsp sunflower oil

In a frying pan, cook the chicken in 2 tablespoons of the oil and when it has cooled down, slice it neatly.

Heat another tablespoon of oil and sauté the spring onions and the garlic for a couple of minutes, taking care that the garlic doesn't brown.

Peel the mangoes and cut them into thick matchsticks. Cut the unpeeled apple into thick matchsticks.

For the dressing, mix the fish sauce, sugar, zest and the juice of the limes and the oil together, then check for seasoning – you may need just a little more sugar.

Put the chicken, chillies, spring onions, garlic, herbs and rocket or watercress on a serving plate with the mangoes and the apple, pour over the dressing and mix well.

Serve with the peanuts scattered on top.

Chicken with Lime & Mint

SERVES 4

A good dish for a hot summer's evening, this is light and fresh and requires almost no time at all in the kitchen. Having said that, the chopping involved is time consuming, but I have discovered that the task becomes much less arduous if shared with willing guests around a garden table, a glass of wine in hand.

3 boneless, skinless
  chicken breasts,
  thinly sliced
7 tbsp sunflower oil
6 spring onions,
  finely chopped
6 garlic cloves,
  finely chopped
6cm piece of fresh
  root ginger, grated
6 small red chillies,
  deseeded and
  finely chopped
75g peanuts,
  finely chopped
zest and juice
  of 5 limes
3–4 tbsp fish sauce
a large handful
  of mint leaves,
  finely chopped
a large handful of
  basil leaves, torn

Cook the chicken in 3 tablespoons of the oil in a frying pan until golden. Remove and keep warm.

Add the remaining oil to the pan and heat until very hot.

Cook the spring onions, the garlic, ginger and chillies for a minute or two. Tip in the nuts and cook for another minute or two.

Return the chicken to the pan and stir in the lime juice and zest and the fish sauce and cook for a final two minutes.

Stir in the herbs and serve on Thai rice, cooked according to the instructions on the packet.

Chicken Stuffed with Tapenade

SERVES 4

If you are a purist you can make the tapenade yourself, but then the dish becomes more time consuming – and the point of it is that it is quick and easy. This is also very good cold.

1 pot of tapenade
zest and juice of
  1 lemon
1 garlic clove, crushed
1 tbsp chopped
  parsley
1 really good chicken
1 tbsp olive oil
salt and pepper

Mix the tapenade with the lemon zest, garlic and parsley.

Using your fingers, gently separate the skin from the flesh of the chicken and spoon in the tapenade mixture. Ideally, push it down both the breast and the legs; this is fiddly but not difficult.

Season the skin and pour over the oil and the lemon juice.

Roast at 200°C/Fan 180°C/Gas 6 for 20 minutes per 500g, plus 20 minutes extra.

Serve with mashed potato and the juices. A simple green salad is the only other thing you need.

Smoked Chicken Salad

SERVES 6

Smoked chicken is inexpensive and easy to find in supermarkets in France; I always have one in the freezer because it makes a quick and easy lunch and the bones make a really wonderful stock. This is really just an idea for a salad – you could use chargrilled chicken breasts and any salad leaves as long as they are robust ones. Also, you could substitute sugar snaps for the beans and artichoke bottoms for the hearts.

a large handful of French beans, topped and tailed
6 red onions, cut into slices about 2cm thick
1 tbsp olive oil
1 smoked chicken, flesh removed and cut into chunks
1 jar of artichoke hearts in olive oil, each one cut in half
1 radicchio or failing that, red chicory
2 tbsp toasted pine nuts
1 tbsp chopped tarragon
balsamic vinegar to taste
salt and pepper

Cook the beans so that they retain some crunch.

Lay out the red onion slices in a roasting tin, drizzle with olive oil and cook at 200°C/ Fan 180°C/Gas 6 for 30–40 minutes until they are just beginning to char.

Combine the chicken, the beans, the artichokes and the radicchio or red chicory, and pour over the olive oil from the onions and from the jar of artichokes. Drizzle with balsamic vinegar, season and mix well.

Top with the pine nuts and the tarragon.

Spatchcock Chicken with Couscous

SERVES 4

Your butcher will always spatchcock a chicken for you but it's very easy to do yourself: using really good kitchen scissors, cut along the spine and open the chicken out flat. This is a fantastically easy dish and very nearly as good cooked in the oven as it is on the barbecue. The perfect accompaniment is some simple couscous.

1 tbsp cumin seeds
1 tsp ground coriander
1 tsp ground cumin seeds from 8 cardamom pods
1 tbsp chilli flakes
10 sprigs of thyme
juice of 2 lemons and the zest of 1 of them
2 garlic cloves, crushed
1 tbsp caster sugar
4 tbsp olive oil
1 medium chicken
1 chicken stock cube
250g couscous
100g rocket
salt and pepper

Combine the cumin, coriander, cardamom, chilli, thyme leaves, zest and juice of 1 lemon (keep the shells), garlic, sugar and olive oil.

Put the chicken in a foil-lined tin, spread the marinade all over it, tuck the lemon shells underneath, and leave for as long as you can – overnight is fine.

Cook at 220°C/Fan 200°C/Gas 7 for 45 minutes (the timings are the same on the barbecue).

Meanwhile, add a chicken stock cube to the couscous and cover it with boiling water, making sure the stock cube dissolves.

When the chicken is cooked, pour any juices left in the pan into the couscous and stir in the rest of the lemon juice and the rocket. Add salt and pepper to taste.

Asian Beef Salad

SERVES 8

This is a dish for a dinner party and although fillet is expensive,
you need surprisingly little of it, so this is not as extravagant
as it sounds. It is perfect for a hot summer's evening.

500g fillet of beef
olive oil
2 carrots
6 spring onions
a small bunch of
  mint leaves
a handful of coriander
100g salted peanuts
2 tbsp sesame seeds
4 limes, to serve
4 large handfuls of
  mixed salad leaves
3 large handfuls of
  beansprouts
salt and pepper

Dressing
5cm piece of fresh root
  ginger, finely chopped
2 red chillies, deseeded
  and finely sliced
1 garlic clove, crushed
4 tbsp sesame oil
juice and zest of 3 limes
2 tbsp fish sauce
2 tbsp soy sauce
2 tbsp rice wine vinegar
3 tsp soft brown sugar

Heat a griddle pan (or a barbecue) until very hot, rub the beef with olive oil and sear it on all sides. It is meant to be very rare, so I cook it for about 2–3 minutes on each side.

When the beef is cold, slice it as thinly as possible.

Peel and cut the carrots into fine matchsticks, finely slice the spring onions, tear up the mint leaves and roughly chop the coriander and the peanuts. Toast the sesame seeds and cut the lime into quarters.

Mix the dressing ingredients together.

Mix the salad leaves, beansprouts, carrots, spring onions and herbs and pile them up in the centre of a large dish. Then arrange the slices of beef around the edges and drizzle the dressing over everything. Sprinkle over the sesame seeds and some of the peanuts, putting the rest of them separately in a bowl to hand round.

Serve with wedges of lime.

Fillet of Beef with Dried Mushrooms

SERVES 6

I don't use grand dried mushrooms for this: it's not worth it. Instead I buy a packet of mixed varieties available in any French supermarket at a fraction of the price of the ones in England. Pulverised in a food processor, they become a wonderful smelling dust and make a fillet of beef even more of a treat. The recipe works just as well with pork fillet, as long as you alter the cooking time to 20–30 minutes, depending on whether you like a faintly pink middle or not.

1 tsp black
  peppercorns
30g dried mushrooms
1kg fillet of beef,
  cut so that it's all
  the same thickness
olive oil

Put the peppercorns and mushrooms into a food processor and grind to a powder.

Roll the beef in the mushroom powder and brown it all over in the olive oil. If it suits, you can do all this the day before as long as you bring the meat up to room temperature before you cook it.

If you are going to serve the beef hot, roast at 220°C/Fan 200°C/Gas 7 for 20 minutes for rare or 25 minutes for medium rare and allow it to rest for 10–15 minutes before slicing.

If you want to serve the beef cold, I would suggest you cook it on an oiled griddle, browning it for about 3 minutes on every side. It will be very rare, but this way you really can get everything done in advance.

Pork Fillet Medallions

SERVES 6

*A dinner party recipe, but one that can be done hours ahead,
apart from the final cooking, and which looks rather more
sophisticated than it actually is. I often serve it with my
Carrot Purée (see page 82), as that negates the need
for gravy, and some crisp green beans.*

1 tsp chopped
   rosemary
1 beaten egg
1kg pork fillet
1 tbsp plain flour
150g chopped
   hazelnuts
50g butter
1 tbsp olive oil
salt and pepper

Mix the rosemary and the egg together
and leave for as long as possible so that the
rosemary infuses the egg. If you don't have
time, don't worry.

Trim the fat off the pork and cut off both
the ends so you have a neat-looking piece of
meat (keep the ends to use on another occasion).

Season the flour and roll the fillet first in
the flour and then in the egg mixture. Finally
roll the fillet in the hazelnuts.

Cut the meat into 6 slices, each 3cm thick.
They should stand up like little barrels.

Brown each one in the butter and oil
mixture on the nut-free ends only and then
transfer to a roasting tin.

Cook at 200°C/Fan 180°C/Gas 6 for
10 minutes.

Stuffed Pork Fillet

SERVES 4

Here are three fillings with which to stuff your fillet before wrapping it in bacon. The Salsa Truffina elevates the pork to a dinner party dish and is simply delicious (see below). The pesto filling is rather more summery than the others, and the prunes root the dish very much in Southwest France. I serve this either with the Potatoes in Mushroom Stock (see page 94) or with the Haricots Blancs (see page 96), as these vegetables provide the 'gravy' that is needed.

1 plump pork fillet,
sinews removed
12 slices of smoked
streaky bacon
olive oil

MUSHROOM DUXELLES FILLING

Take a shallot, 15g of dried mushrooms soaked in 100ml boiling water, 250g of fresh mushrooms, roughly chopped, and a large glug of Madeira.

Cook the shallots in butter till soft, add the fresh mushrooms and cook over a high heat for 5 minutes. Tip in the dried mushrooms, their soaking water and the Madeira and cook over a high heat till the liquid has all but evaporated.

Transfer to a food processor and pulse till you have a rough paste. Or use a jar of L'Aquila Salsa Truffina – quicker, easier and very much better than anything I can make.

Nota Bene
You can buy Salsa Truffina online. It is one of the very few things I always have in my store cupboard as it has endless uses.

PESTO FILLING

Whizz 80g of basil, a garlic clove, 50g of pine nuts, 50g of grated Parmesan and 150ml of olive oil in a food processor in a food processor. Or buy as good-quality pesto as you can find in a tub, never a jar. You could also use sundried tomato purée or tapenade.

PRUNE FILLING

After removing their stones, soak 10 prunes d'Agen in Armagnac overnight.

STUFFING THE FILLET

Cut almost but not quite through the pork fillet, open it out and beat it until flat.

On a baking tray, lay out the bacon in a long line, just overlapping, and put the pork fillet on top. Spread the pork with the filling you have chosen and then, holding the two edges of the pork together, wrap the bacon around it. It's easier to do this starting from the end that you finished laying out the bacon.

Turn the pork upside down so that the seam is underneath, drizzle with a little olive oil and cook at 200°C/Fan 180°C/Gas 6 for 40 minutes. Serve cut into 8 thick slices.

Tagliatelle with Butter & Spices

SERVES 4

This is the recipe I fall back on when our guests have gone, I have completely run out of ideas and the fridge is empty; all the ingredients are ones you will have in the store cupboard. If you happen to have any parsley, sprinkle it over the pasta before serving.

10 shallots,
  chopped finely
200g butter
3 tbsp olive oil
1 tsp ground ginger
1 tsp paprika
1 tsp ground
  coriander
1 tsp ground
  cinnamon
1 tsp turmeric
1 tsp chilli flakes
350g tagliatelle
100g toasted
  pine nuts
salt and pepper

Cook the shallots gently in the butter and oil for 10–15 minutes until they are really soft.

When the butter begins to turn brown and smell nutty, add all the spices and season generously with salt and pepper

Cook the tagliatelle in really well salted water, according to instructions on the packet. Drain and pour the spiced butter over it. Top with the pine nuts.

Nota bene
An Italian friend of mine once told me that the secret to her pasta was to put a large handful of salt into the boiling water: she said the water 'must taste of the sea'.

Lamb Fillet with Potatoes & Red Pepper Sauce

SERVES 6

This is a dish bursting with Mediterranean flavours; the slightly unusual combination of olives and potatoes works surprisingly well and, with the red pepper sauce, elevates plain roast meat to a different level. If you want a vegetable to accompany it, I would suggest Courgette Ribbons (see page 91).

100ml olive oil
3 lamb neck fillets
zest and juice of
 1 lemon
2 tsp capers
2 tbsp chopped
 rosemary
2 tbsp chopped
 parsley
1 garlic clove, crushed
2 tbsp sundried
 tomato purée

Red pepper sauce
3 red peppers, halved
 and deseeded
250ml Greek yoghurt
30g basil leaves,
 roughly torn

Heat a tablespoon of the oil in a pan and sear the lamb fillets until golden on all sides.

Combine the remaining oil with the lemon zest and juice, capers, herbs, garlic and tomato purée to make a rough paste. Smear this mixture all over the lamb and leave it to absorb the flavours for as long as possible – it will happily sit overnight.

Roast the peppers in an oven preheated to 200°C/Fan 180°C/Gas 6 for about 30 minutes or until the skins are nicely blackened. Put the peppers in a plastic bag and leave them to cool. Don't be tempted to use the roasted peppers you can buy in a jar.

When the peppers are cool enough to handle, peel and slice them and mix – together with any juices which have accumulated in the bag – into the yoghurt, along with the roughly torn basil leaves. Season well. *Continued overleaf*

Potatoes
500g new potatoes
120g black olives,
    roughly chopped
50ml olive oil
salt and pepper

Cook the potatoes until tender, then drain and crush roughly with a fork. Mix them with the olives and the 50ml of olive oil and season well.

While the potatoes are cooking, roast the lamb for 15 minutes in an oven preheated to 200°C/Fan 180°C/Gas 6.

Slice the lamb and serve on a mound of potatoes with the red pepper sauce alongside.

Nota Bene
Rather than using pitted olives, which never taste as good, remove the stones from olives and chop roughly.

Cod, Lentils & Sauce Verte

SERVES 4

When I am in France, I use the local jambon de Bayonne for this recipe, but in England, I use Serrano ham as it's cheaper than Parma ham and works just as well. This is a useful recipe as everything, other than the final cooking of the fish, can be done hours ahead.

4 pieces of cod loin
8 slices of jambon
  de Bayonne
  (or Serrano ham)
230g Puy lentils
1 litre chicken stock
1 garlic clove, peeled
  and cut in half
1 bay leaf
1 small onion, peeled
  and cut in half
salt and pepper

Sauce verte
a large handful
  of parsley
a small handful each
  of mint and basil
2 garlic cloves
1 tbsp Dijon mustard
4 anchovy fillets
1 tbsp capers, rinsed
150ml strong olive oil

Wrap each portion of cod in a couple of slices of ham and cook it in olive oil until it is golden on both sides. Then transfer to a roasting tin.

Cook the lentils in chicken stock (a stock cube is fine for this) with the onion, bay leaf and garlic for about 20 minutes, until they are soft but still have a bit of bite. Remove the garlic, onion and bay leaf. Season the lentils really well and possibly add a splash of balsamic vinegar or of concentrated liquid stock.

If you are short of time, use ready-cooked lentils but season them well so that they aren't too bland.

For the sauce verte, whizz up the herbs, mustard, garlic, anchovies and capers in a food processor, pouring the oil in slowly and seasoning well. Put into a bowl to serve.

Cook the fish at 200°C/Fan 180°C/ Gas 6 for 10 minutes. Serve with the lentils and the bowl of sauce verte.

Cod in Seconds

SERVES 4

*This is hardly a recipe, more a reminder of what you can
do in a matter of seconds when you are tired but still have
a houseful of hungry guests.*

4 tsp fresh thyme
  leaves
2 tsp chilli flakes
zest of 2 lemons,
  grated
4 pieces of cod loin
olive oil
salt and pepper

Mix together the thyme, chilli and lemon zest
and season really well. Pat the mixture on top
of the cod and drizzle with a little oil.

Cook for 10 minutes at 220°C/Fan 200°C/
Gas 7.

I like to serve this dish with Roasted Pepper
Salad (see page 24) and Couscous with Herbs
(see page 34).

Salmon & Prawns
on Parsley Rice

SERVES 6

This is a very pretty summery dish and one you can make hours in advance. I always make mayonnaise by hand because the family far prefer it to the kind made in a food processor – the consistency is completely different, richer and less gelatinous. For this recipe you can use whichever you prefer; the only mayonnaise that simply won't do, is the bought kind, however grand it is.

4 salmon steaks
(or a large trout
if you prefer)
200g basmati rice
a large bunch of
parsley, chopped
very finely (I do this
in a food processor)
a small handful of
chopped dill
about 500ml
homemade
mayonnaise
(see page 172)
200g extra-large king
prawns, peeled
and cooked
salt and pepper

If you are using salmon steaks, poach them in boiling water for 5–8 minutes. The exact timing entirely depends on how thick they are, but as soon as they are opaque, remove them and leave to cool. When they are cold, remove the skin.

If you are using a trout, oil a large rectangle of foil, place the fish on it with a squeeze of lemon juice and wrap it up. Bake at 170°C/ Fan 150°C/Gas 3 for 20–30 minutes – you will be able to smell it when it's ready. Open the foil packet, leave the fish to cool and then take it off the bone, keeping it in as large pieces as possible.

Wash the rice in cold water before cooking it. As soon as the rice is done, run it under the cold tap to stop it from continuing to cook. Season really well and then stir in all the parsley so that the rice looks more green than white.

Add the dill to the mayonnaise and check the seasoning. Then carefully stir the fish and the prawns into the mayonnaise, making sure that everything is well coated; you need a surprising amount of mayonnaise, as the rice is dry.

To serve, arrange the rice in a circle on a serving dish and spoon the fish and prawns into the middle.

Tuna

SERVES 4

Cooked on a barbecue, this is delicious but a griddle will do just as well — you just can't delegate the cooking so easily. I usually cook this in the summer and serve it, very simply, with a green salad, dressed with sesame oil, but if it's chilly, or you want something more substantial, serve it with noodles to which you have added sesame oil.

5 tbsp vegetable oil
8 tbsp soy sauce
2 tbsp soft light brown sugar
4 tuna steaks
4 shallots, finely sliced
3 red chillies, deseeded and finely chopped
2 garlic cloves, crushed
3cm piece of fresh root ginger, peeled and grated
1 tbsp fish sauce
juice of 3 limes
40g peanuts, coarsely chopped
2 tbsp chopped coriander leaves

Mix 2 tablespoons of the oil with the soy sauce and a tablespoon of the sugar and leave the tuna to marinate in this for 30 minutes

Heat a tablespoon of oil and gently fry the shallots till they are soft. Add the chillies, garlic and ginger and cook for a couple of minutes.

Add the remaining tablespoon of sugar and continue to cook till the mixture is beginning to caramelise. Then stir in the fish sauce, the juice of 2 of the limes, the rest of the oil, the peanuts and the coriander.

Cook the tuna on either a barbecue or a griddle for 1½ minutes on each side. Squeeze the juice of the remaining lime over each steak.

Serve with the shallot mixture piled on top of the tuna and some noodles, as suggested above, if you like.

DINNER
PUDDINGS

I love puddings – I love making them and I love eating them, but most of all I love their prettiness and inventiveness, the way they fill the house with the smell of warm sugar and finish a meal with a flourish. However, they need be neither complicated nor time consuming and this selection of recipes proves the point.

Orange & Passion Fruit Tart

SERVES 6-8

This tart is very little trouble — and it's delicious — but I always feel it looks a bit dreary. When I have time, I decorate it with roasted orange slices but it really is not necessary and although it looks good, it does make the tart difficult to cut. An easier alternative would be to decorate the tart with crystallised peel.

Pastry
115g butter
140g plain flour
30g icing sugar

Filling
6 passion fruit
350ml orange juice
40g dark chocolate (70%)
250g caster sugar
200ml double cream
5 medium eggs
1 egg yolk

Optional decoration
2 oranges
juice of 3 oranges
100g caster sugar

Put all the pastry ingredients in a food processor and mix until the dough forms a ball. Press the dough into a 23cm tart tin with and the dough will only just fit the tin). Prick the pastry over really thoroughly, even up the sides (this will prevent shrinkage), then chill in the fridge.

Cook the tart case in a preheated oven at 180°C/Fan 160°C/Gas 4 for 15 minutes or until golden. Remove it from the oven and reduce the temperature to 150°C/Fan 130°C/Gas 2.

Scoop the pulp and the seeds of the passion fruit into a saucepan, then add the orange juice, bring to the boil and reduce by half. You should have about 250ml. Set aside to cool.

Melt the chocolate in a bowl placed over a pan of simmering water. Using a pastry brush, paint the inside of the tart case with melted chocolate. Leave to chill until the chocolate is completely set.

Beat the reduced fruit juice with the sugar, cream, eggs and egg yolk until the mixture is smooth, then strain through a sieve into a jug.

Put the tart tin on a baking tray in the oven, pulling the shelf out as far as you can with safety. Carefully pour the filling into the pastry case (it will reach the very top) and gently push the shelf back in.

Cook for 35–40 minutes, remove from the oven and allow to cool in the tin. It will firm up as it cools, so don't worry if it's slightly soft in the centre when you take it out of the oven.

If decorating with orange, cut the oranges into thin slices, discarding the ends, put them on a baking tray, then sprinkle with the orange juice and the caster sugar. Cover with foil and roast at 180°C/Fan 160°C/Gas 4 for 1 hour. Uncover and continue to cook for 30–40 minutes until all the juice has evaporated and the slices are just a little singed. Cool on greaseproof paper and use to decorate the tart.

Serve the tart with crème fraîche.

Nota Bene
Tubs of very good crystallised orange peel can be bought in any French supermarket and make a nice decoration for the tart.

Orange & Raspberry Cake

SERVES 8

This wonderful cake is based on Diana Henry's recipe but she uses ingredients I can't find in rural French supermarkets. It keeps well for a day or two, although in our house it never has the chance. I have used both raspberry and peach juice with equal success and I always decorate the cake with whichever fruit I have chosen for the syrup.

Cake
50g fine white
  breadcrumbs
100g ground almonds
175g soft light
  brown sugar
2 tsp baking powder
zest of 1½ oranges
215ml light olive oil
4 eggs, beaten
raspberries or peaches,
  to decorate

Syrup
juice of 1 orange
100ml pure raspberry
  or peach juice
3 tbsp runny honey

Grease a 20cm cake tin with a removable base and line it with baking parchment.

Mix all the cake ingredients together and pour the batter into the tin. Put it in a cold oven that you then set to 190°C/Fan 170°C/Gas 5. After 40 minutes test the cake with a skewer. If it doesn't come out clean, leave the cake in the oven for another 5 minutes but no more.

While the cake is cooking, make the syrup by boiling down the orange juice, peach or raspberry juice and the honey. You want to have about 100ml of reduced syrup.

As soon as the cake is out of the oven, make holes all over it with a skewer and pour the syrup slowly on to it. The cake usually sinks in the middle but by the time you have decorated it with whichever fruit you choose, no one will notice.

Serve with crème fraîche.

Apricot Tart

SERVES 6

You can use more or less any fruit for this – figs and plums are particularly good – but apricot remains a great favourite. I have frozen this tart but I always regret it; it's not a time-consuming recipe and tastes infinitely better made on the day you are eating it.

Pastry
110g butter
140g plain flour
30g icing sugar

Filling
125g butter
125g ground almonds
125g caster sugar
1 egg
8 apricots, halved
   and stoned

Glaze
3 tbsp apricot jam
1 tbsp lemon juice

Put all the pastry ingredients in a food processor and mix until the dough forms a ball. Press the dough into a 23cm tart tin with a removable base (the pastry is meant to be thin and the dough will only just fit the tin). Prick the pastry over really thoroughly, even up the sides (this will prevent shrinkage), then chill in the fridge.

Cook in a preheated oven at 180°C/Fan 160°C/Gas 4 for 15 minutes or until golden.

Put the butter, ground almonds and sugar in a food processor and whizz everything up for a few seconds before adding the egg. Whizz it all up again to combine and pour the mixture into the cooked tart case.

Decorate with the apricots, arranging them cut side down, and cook at 180°C/Fan 160°C/Gas 4 for 40 minutes or until the top is golden and beginning to singe.

Boil up the jam and lemon juice for a couple of minutes until it thickens and then glaze the tart while it is still warm. It's important to loosen the tart from the tin while it is still warm or it will get hopelessly stuck.

Fruit Salads

As a child, I always thought fruit salads a second-rate
sort of a pudding, probably because no chocolate is involved.
My attitude to them all these years later is not very different,
but they do have certain advantages: they are quick,
beautiful and not in the least bit bad for one.

PINEAPPLE

This is no more than a reminder of how to transform a pineapple, either for a pudding or for breakfast.

Cut a pineapple into chunks and combine it with the zest and the juice of 2 limes.

Or sprinkle it with lots of mint. Or squeeze the seeds and juice of 4 passion fruit over it.

MANGO

This is a beautiful fruit salad.

Chop up a mango and add it to a handful of blueberries, the seeds of a pomegranate and the juice of a lime.

PEACHES

Cut peaches into segments, arrange them on a dish and drizzle over a jar of raspberry coulis, available in any supermarket.

Walnut Tart

SERVES 4 GENEROUSLY

*This is very much a part of Le Rouzet menus in the early autumn,
when our walnuts are beginning to ripen and every tree seems to
have a red squirrel perched in it, noisily eating our supply. It's like
a sophisticated treacle tart, but not heavy, and is really worth making
even if you don't have large quantities of walnuts to use up.*

Pastry
110g butter
140g flour
30g icing sugar

Filling
20g butter
200g golden syrup
100g walnut halves
a pinch of mixed spice
100g mixed peel
 (see note on page 135)
4 madeleines (or soft
 amaretti), crumbled
1 egg, beaten

Put all the ingredients for the pastry into a food processor and mix until the dough forms a ball. Press the dough into a 20cm tart tin with a removable base. Prick the pastry all over really thoroughly, even up the sides (this will prevent shrinkage), then chill in the fridge.

Cook in a preheated oven at 180°C/Fan 160°C/Gas 4 for 15 minutes or until golden.

Melt the butter and syrup in a pan and stir in all the other ingredients. Pour into the pastry case and cook at 190°C/Fan 170°C/Gas 5 for 15 minutes.

Cool in the tin but as soon as you can, loosen the edges of the tart or it will get stuck. Serve with crème fraîche.

Gipsy Tart

SERVES 8–10

Originally from Kent, this is a very old-fashioned pudding, incredibly sweet but irresistible served with crème fraîche. The secret is to whisk the filling until you have a thick, billowing mousse, which will take a good 15 minutes – don't be tempted to stint on this.

Pastry
110g butter
140g plain flour
30g icing sugar

Filling
205ml evaporated milk
200g dark muscovado
   sugar

Put all the ingredients for the pastry into a food processor and mix until the dough forms a ball. Press the dough into a 23cm tart tin with a removable base (there will be just enough dough to do this). Prick the pastry all over really thoroughly, even up the sides (this will prevent shrinkage), then chill in the fridge.

Cook in a preheated oven at 180°C/ Fan 160°C/Gas 4 for about 20 minutes or until golden.

While the pastry is cooking, put the evaporated milk and the sugar into a bowl and, using an electric mixer, whisk on high speed for 15 minutes. My Kenwood mixer doesn't seem to do the job as well as my hand-held mixer and although this is very tedious, it is absolutely essential.

Pour the filling into the tart case and bake for 10–15 minutes. There will be a few bubbles on the surface, which will be set.

Leave to cool in the tin. Serve with crème fraîche.

Chocolate Tart

SERVES 12

This is based on a recipe by Jamie Oliver and it is our younger son, William's, favourite pudding, so much so that I made dozens for the wedding dinner when he and Katie were married. It is still an essential part of every summer and we all have to bring golden syrup out from England, since it is not easy to find in our part of France!

Pastry
220g butter
280g plain flour
60g icing sugar

Filling
140g butter
160g dark
  chocolate (70%)
8 tbsp cocoa powder
4 large eggs
230g caster sugar
3 tbsp golden syrup
3 heaped tbsp
  crème fraîche

Put all the ingredients for the pastry into a food processor and mix until the dough forms a ball. Press the dough into a 25cm tart tin with a removable base. Prick all over really thoroughly, even up the sides (this will prevent shrinkage), then chill in the fridge. You may have more pastry than you need, but it freezes well. Cook in a preheated oven at 180°C/Fan 160°C/Gas 4 for 15 minutes or until golden.

Melt the butter, chocolate and cocoa powder in a bowl placed over a pan of simmering water.

Beat the eggs and sugar till pale and then add the golden syrup and the crème fraîche.

Stir this into the chocolate mixture and pour it all into the tart case.

Cook at 150°C/Fan 130°C/Gas 2 for 45 minutes. Cool in the tin on a rack for at least an hour, then serve with crème fraîche.

This freezes beautifully.

Baked Chocolate Mousse

SERVES 6

Our elder son John and his wife Tessa chose this pudding, a delicious and easy recipe I have been making at Le Rouzet for years, for their wedding dinner. I always used to serve it with crème fraîche but they vastly improved it by serving it with Honeycomb Ice Cream (see pages 156–7). The two together make a wonderful combination.

150g butter, plus extra for greasing
150g caster sugar
3 large eggs, separated
150g dark chocolate (70%)
icing sugar, to serve

Grease a 20cm loose-bottomed cake tin.

Beat the 150g of butter and sugar till pale. Beat in the egg yolks.

Melt the chocolate in a bowl placed over a pan of simmering water. When the chocolate has cooled slightly, add it to the butter mixture.

Beat the egg whites until they are stiff and fold them gently into the chocolate mixture.

Pour the mixture into the cake tin and bake for an hour at 170°C/Fan 150°C/Gas 3. Leave it to cool in the tin on a rack and when ready to serve, turn it out and dust it with icing sugar.

Chocolate & Salted Caramel Tart

SERVES 10

If you can find it, use dulce de leche but if not, a tin of Nestlé caramel condensed milk will work almost as well. In both cases, stir in a teaspoon of sea salt flakes. This is a rich and splendid pudding.

Pastry
110g butter
140g plain flour
30g icing sugar

Caramel
400g jar of dulce
  de leche or a 397g
  tin of caramel
  condensed milk
1 tsp sea salt flakes

Chocolate
130g dark
  chocolate (70%)
85g butter
1 egg, plus 2
  extra yolks
3 tbsp caster sugar

Put all the ingredients for the pastry into a food processor and mix until the dough forms a ball. Press the dough into a 23cm tart tin with a removable base. Prick all over really thoroughly, even up the sides (this will prevent shrinkage), then chill in the fridge.

Cook in a preheated oven at 200°C/ Fan 180°C/Gas 6 for 15–20 minutes or until golden. Reduce the oven temperature to 180°C/Fan 160°C/Gas 4.

When the pastry has cooled, spread it with the dulce de leche or condensed milk and sprinkle with the sea salt.

Melt the chocolate and butter in a bowl placed over a pan of simmering water. Whisk the egg and the 2 yolks with the sugar until thick and then fold in the chocolate mixture. Pour this mixture over the layer of caramel and bake for 12 minutes.

Serve with crème fraîche.

Elegant Chocolate Mousse

SERVES 6-8

I feel rather embarrassed including a recipe for chocolate mousse, as everyone has their own favourite. However, mine has the virtue of being incredibly easy and, if you take just a bit of extra trouble, also extremely elegant. It's delicious served in thin slices with a cream sauce (see page 148) or as part of a Three-Coloured Chocolate Mousse (see page 148). The cream sauce is not a sauce at all: it's a complete fake made of under-whipped cream that looks and tastes like a crème anglais. I encourage you to try the Three-Coloured Chocolate Mousse; it's not a great deal of work, it looks wonderful and freezes well.

Chocolate mousse
oil, for greasing
285g dark chocolate
  (70%) plus 30g
115g unsalted butter
2 tsp powdered
  instant coffee
  dissolved in 2 tsp
  of boiling water
4 eggs, separated
¼ tsp cream
  of tartar
2 tbsp caster sugar

Prepare either a loaf tin or a 20cm cake tin with a loose base by lightly oiling the bottom and sides. Then, using baking parchment, trace the bottom of the tin and weigh the paper down on a baking sheet (this is to stop it curling).

Melt the 30g of chocolate in a bowl placed over a pan of simmering water and then spread it out over your traced shape. Put this in the fridge for 10 minutes to set.

When the chocolate is hard, very gently peel the paper away from the chocolate and place it in the tin. It will end up as the top of the pudding.

Melt the 285g of chocolate and the butter together in a bowl placed over a saucepan of simmering water. *Continued overleaf*

When melted, stir in the coffee mixture and whisk in the yolks. Cool.

Whisk the egg whites and the cream of tartar until soft peaks form, then gradually add the sugar and continue to beat till the whites are stiff.

Fold a tablespoonful of the egg white mixture into the chocolate to lighten it, followed by the rest until everything is thoroughly incorporated.

Pour the mousse into your prepared tin and leave in the fridge for 4 hours to set. You can make this a day in advance.

When you are ready to serve the mousse, turn it out so that the piece of set chocolate is on the top. Serve with the cream sauce.

CREAM SAUCE

480ml double cream
3–4 tbsp caster sugar
1 tsp vanilla extract

Whip the double cream with the caster sugar and vanilla extract until just beginning to thicken: it should be a voluptuous, thick liquid. You can make this a few hours ahead. If it should separate, just whisk it all together again.

THREE-COLOURED CHOCOLATE MOUSSE

225g good-quality
  milk chocolate
4 tsp instant
  coffee powder
720ml double cream
225g good-quality
  white chocolate

This recipe makes enough for two puddings in 20cm tins. Follow the instructions for the Chocolate Mousse on the previous page, including the chocolate disc. Divide the mixture between the cake tins. Keep them in the fridge while you make the next layer.

Melt the milk chocolate with the instant coffee and 80ml of hot water in a bowl placed over a pan of simmering water.

Whip 360ml of the double cream until soft peaks form and fold it into the cooled chocolate mixture. Divide between the tins and put them back in the fridge.

Melt the white chocolate with 80ml of hot water in a bowl placed over a saucepan of simmering water.

Whip rest of the cream until soft peaks form and fold in the cooled chocolate mixture. Divide between the tins and put them in the fridge.

To unmould, carefully ease away from the sides of the cake tin and turn upside down onto a serving dish so that you have the chocolate disc on the top. You can do all this the day before or freeze the puddings. I serve this just as it is − I don't think it needs a sauce.

Nota bene
Another way to lift an ordinary chocolate mousse is to serve it with a bit of praline scattered over the top.

Take 300g of toasted flaked almonds, 200g of caster sugar and 4 tablespoons of water.

Cook the sugar and water over a medium heat, watching carefully. When the mixture turns golden brown, tip in the nuts. Turn out on to baking parchment and when the praline is cold, either break it into shards or pulse in a food processor until you get small chunks.

If you happen to overprocess it, the praline will turn to powder but it's still extremely good and can be sprinkled over all sorts of puddings. It will keep in an airtight container for a week but not for much longer than that.

Marzipan Bread & Butter Pudding

SERVES 8

Please don't be put off by the fact that this is an old-fashioned pudding; the addition of marzipan transforms it. When I am in France I use stale croissants, as they produce a lighter pudding. In an attempt to make this look more sophisticated, I cut individual circles (with a sharp biscuit cutter) from the baking dish to serve.

100g butter, plus extra for greasing
8 thick slices of white bread, crusts removed, or 8 croissants, cut into chunks
4 eggs
50g caster sugar
350ml milk
100ml double cream
1 vanilla pod
500g ready-to-roll golden marzipan
a handful of sultanas
25g flaked almonds

Grease a baking dish and butter both sides of the bread. (If you use croissants you don't need to butter them.)

In a large bowl whisk the eggs and sugar together until they are smooth.

Bring the milk, cream and vanilla pod to the boil. Then remove the vanilla pod and, using an electric hand-held whisk, slowly pour the milk mixture on to the eggs and sugar.

Roll out the marzipan to fit the dish. In the bottom of the dish, put a layer of bread, followed by the marzipan and sultanas and finally top this with the remaining bread.

Pour over the custard and leave to stand for at least 10 minutes. This is a very forgiving pudding and I have left it for hours without it coming to any harm.

Before cooking, sprinkle on the almonds and bake at 200°C/Fan 180°C/Gas 6 for 30 minutes.

Individual Strawberry Soufflés

SERVES 4

*Throughout the summer I make large quantities of mayonnaise which
means that I have a constant supply of egg whites; this is a favourite
way of using up quite a lot of them in one go. It's the easiest soufflé
ever invented and it can wait for hours in the fridge before you cook it.*

500g strawberries
2 tbsp lemon juice
80g icing sugar
5 egg whites
200g good-quality
   white chocolate
200g double cream

Nota Bene
If by any chance,
the sauce mixture
catches on the bottom
of the saucepan, don't
worry, as the little
bits of caramelised
chocolate, while
not very decorative,
are delicious.

Line a baking sheet with baking parchment,
place the strawberries on it and cook them
at 180°C/Fan 160°C/Gas 4 for 15 minutes
or until they become soft and juicy.

Put them in a food processor and whizz
them up, then push them through a sieve.

Beat in the lemon juice and the icing sugar.

Whisk the egg whites until they are stiff and
then fold in the strawberry purée very gently.

Generously butter 4 ramekin dishes and
pour the strawberry mixture into them, piling
the mixture as high as you can. Put the ramekins
in the fridge until you are ready to cook them.

For the sauce, break the white chocolate
into small pieces and add it to the cream in
a pan. Heat this mixture very slowly, stirring
till it amalgamates.

Heat the oven to 180°C/Fan 160°C/
Gas 4 and cook the soufflés for 12–15 minutes
until the tops are gently browned.

Make a hole in the top of each soufflé
and pour in the white chocolate sauce.

Individual Lemon Soufflés

SERVES 6

These soufflés are wonderfully easy because they can sit in the fridge for hours before baking. You can use any curd – raspberry and passion fruit are particularly good – but in that case leave out the Limoncello.

butter, for greasing
325g jar of the best lemon curd you can find (cheaper varieties tend to be too sweet)
zest of 1 lemon, finely grated
6 egg whites
a pinch of cream of tartar
60g caster sugar
2 tbsp Limoncello

Butter 6 ramekins well.

Warm the lemon curd and zest very gently in a small pan. Then whip the egg whites and the cream of tartar until you have billowing soft peaks. Whisk in the sugar.

Mix the Limoncello into the lemon curd and then fold in the whites. Spoon into the ramekins and put the soufflés into the fridge until you are ready to cook them.

Preheat the oven to 200°C/Fan 180°C/ Gas 6 and bake the soufflés for 12 minutes.

Carmelle – a Cheat's Pudding

*This is the ultimate cheat's pudding and stems from a tip
given to me by my sister-in-law, Jan.*

Buy a packet of Carmelle, a small (and very cheap) pudding made
by Greens which you will find in any English supermarket, generally
in the section selling rice pudding, tart cases and coulis.

Pay no attention to the instructions on the packet and make them
up substituting the milk with double cream.

You can pour this mixture into ramekins, glaze the top and
pretend it is crème brûlée. Or you can call it panna cotta and serve
it with a fruit coulis (bought in the same section of the supermarket
as the Carmelle) or with the delicious caramel syrup you find in all
French shops (the packet of Carmelle actually comes with a small
sachet of this syrup).

Alternatively you can make a sweet pastry case, fill it with the
Carmelle mixture and caramelise the top (see below). It then becomes
a crème brûlée tart, delicious served with berries.

Another idea is to fill a sweet pastry case with the Carmelle mixture,
made with a spoonful or two less of cream than usual. While the
mixture is still warm, stir in the same amount of elderflower cordial.
When it has set, cover the tart with sliced strawberries.

Nota Bene
I always have Carmelle in the cupboard, as it's an instant solution to the
problem of feeding unexpected guests – incredibly quick and extremely good.
Rather surprisingly, it also lasts in a ramekin in the fridge for a couple of days.

To caramelise the Carmelle, sprinkle caster sugar all over the top and
either put it under the grill or brown it with a blowtorch.

Ice Cream

SERVES 6

I make this ice cream all summer long, ringing the changes with the additions below. If you are really pushed for time, you could always buy good-quality vanilla ice cream, but this recipe is so ridiculously easy that it's a shame not to use it — you don't even have to stir it.

Basic mixture
550ml double cream
397g tin of
   condensed milk
1 tbsp vodka

Whip the cream until it is floppy and then beat in the condensed milk and vodka. Continue whisking until very thick. Freeze.

You could add all sorts of things into the basic mixture, but the following are our family favourites.

WALNUTS

Mix 100g of walnuts with 3 tablespoons of icing sugar and 1 tablespoon of water. Roast for 15 minutes at 170°C/Fan 150°C/Gas 3. When the nuts are cold, stir them into the ice cream and serve with maple syrup or the liquid caramel that you can buy in French supermarkets.

PASSION FRUIT

Scoop the flesh and seeds of 8 passion fruit into the ice cream. Add 2 tablespoons of sieved icing sugar and mix well.

HONEYCOMB

Heat 2 tablespoons of golden syrup and 5 tablespoons of caster sugar over a very low heat until the sugar melts. Then boil rapidly until the caramel is a mid-golden colour. Remove from the heat, sift over 1 teaspoon of bicarbonate of soda and then pour the frothy mixture on to a greased baking sheet.

When it's cold, break into smallish chunks and mix into the ice cream. This works wonderfully well with the baked chocolate mousse.

DULCE DE LECHE

Just swirl this into the frozen ice cream, then refreeze. It's a really good alternative to crème fraîche when you are serving a pear tart or the baked chocolate mousse.

If you can't find dulce de leche, use a tin of caramel condensed milk which most supermarkets stock. The trick here is to add a pinch or two of sea salt; it makes all the difference.

MERINGUES

Because I make so many egg-based sauces, I always have a good supply of egg whites with which to make meringues. Any leftover meringues transform a vanilla ice cream: just crush as many as you happen to have and stir them into the ice cream. Serve with fruit or a fruit coulis.

Espresso Ice Cream

SERVES 12

This is rather a sophisticated ice cream but the work of minutes. If you are really short of time, you don't even need to make the caramel sauce – use a tin of caramel condensed milk or a jar of thick caramel sauce, found in every supermarket. Whatever kind of caramel you use, don't omit the salt; it makes all the difference.

Ice cream
4 tbsp instant espresso coffee powder
600ml double cream
397g tin of condensed milk
Lotus Biscoff biscuits, crushed, to decorate

Caramel
200g caster sugar
200ml double cream
¼ tsp fine sea salt

To make the caramel, dissolve the sugar in 3 tablespoons of water and allow it to bubble till it becomes golden. Pour in the cream and stir the mixture over a low heat till it's all amalgamated. Add the salt and leave to get completely cold.

Dissolve the coffee powder in 2 tablespoons of boiling water and allow to cool.

Whisk the cream with the condensed milk and the cooled coffee mixture until soft peaks have formed.

Put half the ice cream into a container, then pour half of the caramel mixture over it. Repeat and then freeze. Serve sprinkled with the crushed biscuits.

Lemon & Ginger Sorbet

SERVES 8

This recipe, given to me by a friend in France, has become a staple at Le Rouzet, as it is not only incredibly easy, but also wonderfully refreshing on a hot summer's evening.

550g granulated sugar
5cm piece of fresh root ginger, finely grated
440ml lemon juice (about 6 large lemons)
2 tbsp lemon zest, finely grated

Heat 420ml of water with the sugar in a pan until the sugar has completely dissolved.

Remove from the heat and when the syrup is cool, add the ginger, lemon juice and zest. Freeze.

After about 4 hours, or when the mixture is completely frozen, whizz it up in a food processor to break up the ice crystals, then refreeze until you are ready to use it.

A MISCELLANY

A chapter of bits and pieces that don't fit into any other categories, these recipes are none the less important to me, either because family and friends love them (Brownies and Cheese Biscuits in particular) or because they are everyday essentials (Pastry). Some of my favourite and most useful recipes are here.

Pastry

I only make one kind of pastry and it's ridiculously easy. I rarely bother to line the pastry cases, except when using puff pastry; instead, I prick them incredibly thoroughly, and I never have any trouble with shrinkage. If you are sceptical, line the pastry with baking parchment and baking beans, then after 15 minutes, remove the paper and beans and cook for a further 5 minutes to allow the base to dry out.

Shortcrust pastry
110g butter
140g flour
30g strong Cheddar, grated

Nota bene
If you want sweet pastry, substitute 30g icing sugar for the cheese.

Put all the ingredients for the pastry into a food processor and mix until the dough forms a ball. Press the dough into whatever tin you are using (the mixture makes enough – just – for a 23cm tin). Prick all over really thoroughly, even up the sides, to prevent shrinkage, then chill in the fridge.

Cook in a preheated oven at 180°C/Fan 160°C/Gas 4 for 15 minutes or until golden.

The pastry freezes so well that I generally make more than I need.

PUFF PASTRY

I usually use a block (although this is impossible to find in Southwest France so I import it) rather than the ready-rolled puff pastry, which is always rather disappointing. It's best to buy the kind with extra butter, but if you can't find it, roll the ordinary pastry out to about 2cm in thickness, spread it generously with butter, fold it over and roll it out as usual.

My Father's Water Biscuits

Anyone who knew my father would be very surprised by this recipe. Renowned for his cellar and for his appreciation of good food, he was also someone whose culinary skills stretched no further than, on one memorable occasion, grilling a boil-in the-bag kipper while still in its bag. After that, I can't recall him cooking again until I was expecting our eldest son, John, and was feeling unwell; he thought that these water biscuits, a feature of his childhood, might help with the sickness and very touchingly, he kept me supplied throughout both my pregnancies. They are absolutely delicious with or without cheese.

170g plain flour,
  plus extra
  for dusting
1 level tsp baking
  powder
43g butter
140ml milk
salt

Put all the ingredients into a food processor with a large pinch of salt and blend till you have a stiff dough.

Sprinkle a chopping board with flour and salt, divide the dough into 4 and roll it out very, very thinly: my pa would say until the dough is 'practically transparent'. This is really important.

Cut the dough into triangles and put them on a baking sheet lined with baking parchment. If you don't want the biscuits to have air bubbles, then prick them, but personally, I prefer the unevenness and never bother.

Cook at 180°C/Fan 160°C/Gas 4 for about 10 minutes until golden brown. These biscuits keep for a couple of days in the tin, but they are difficult to resist, so we seldom have any left over.

Cheese Biscuits

MAKES 40

I have dozens of recipes for cheese biscuits, but these are the ones the family insist on and I always have some in the freezer, ready to bake.

250g extra-mature
  Cheddar, cut
  into chunks
250g salted butter,
  straight from the
  fridge, cut into
  chunks
250g plain flour
Tabasco
Dijon mustard
salt and pepper

These amounts fit into my food processor perfectly; don't be tempted to do more in one go, as it just won't mix properly.

Put the cheese, butter and flour into the food processor and add 12 shakes of the Tabasco bottle, 1 heaped tablespoon of Dijon mustard, 25 grinds of pepper and 2 teaspoons of salt. (This is just a guide – you can season the mixture as you want, but you will be surprised by the amount you need. The biscuits come out differently every time; it depends how heavy-handed you have been!)

Whizz all this up in a food processor and as soon as the mixture forms a ball, stop and divide it into 3 parts.

Lay out 3 large bits of cling film and put a ball of cheese mixture on to each. With damp hands, roughly shape each ball into a sausage. Then roll up each parcel in the cling film and holding one end tightly, with the other hand, the thumb and first finger forming a circle, ease the dough along the cling film, so you have a long, even sausage measuring about 30cm long and 5cm across. *Continued overleaf*

Freeze these parcels until you are ready
to use them (don't attempt to cut them unless
they are very cold as they will end up squashy).

When you are ready to cook the biscuits,
take the parcels out of the freezer and heat
the oven to 200°C/Fan 180°C/Gas 6.
By the time the oven has reached the right
temperature, the cheese sausages will have
thawed enough to cut into 2cm slices.

Line a tray with baking parchment
and arrange the slices on it. Cook for about
10 minutes until golden brown; you can move
them on to a serving plate straight from the
oven without them coming to any harm.

These are best eaten on the day they
are cooked, but if you have any left over,
they freeze beautifully.

Cheese Puffballs

SERVES 4

These are another way to use up my endless supply of egg whites, and they are particularly popular with children. Having said that, the adults seem to steal as many as the children eat for their supper. You can keep them quite safely in a warm oven for half an hour.

Cheese puffballs
2 egg whites
250g Cheddar
    cheese, grated
white breadcrumbs
sunflower oil
salt and pepper

Sauce
1 onion, finely
    chopped
2 tbsp olive oil
400g tin of chopped
    tomatoes
1 garlic clove, crushed
1 tbsp sundried
    tomato paste
½ tsp caster sugar
a handful of basil
    leaves, torn
salt and pepper

First make the sauce. Cook the onion in the oil until really soft.

Tip in the tomatoes, garlic, tomato paste, caster sugar and basil. Simmer, uncovered, for 30 minutes and then, when the sauce has cooled a little, whizz it up in a food processor and season.

For the puffs, whisk the egg whites to a froth, stir in the cheese and season well.

Roll the cheese paste into walnut-sized balls, cover each one in breadcrumbs and chill well – they need to be really cold, so I usually make them in the morning to use in the evening.

Heat the sunflower oil to a depth of about 5cm and cook the cheese balls two at a time until they are golden and crispy. Drain them on kitchen paper and put them in a warm oven while you cook the others.

Serve with the warmed-up tomato sauce.

French Dressing

Originally this was a dressing I concocted when my husband,
Richard, was on a diet but it's good enough to use even if you are
not worried about your figure. It's my dressing of preference in the
summer when I am producing arrays of salads and therefore
using a great deal of oil.

1 tbsp strong olive oil
5 tbsp good chicken stock
1 small garlic clove, crushed
½ tsp tarragon leaves, very finely chopped
½ tsp parsley, very finely chopped
½ tsp basil leaves, very finely chopped
1 tbsp sherry vinegar
1 tbsp lemon juice

It's a bother to finely chop the herbs, but it's really worth it, as they become part of the dressing rather than an addition to the salad leaves.

Mix everything together and set aside until ready to use.

Mayonnaise

Handmade mayonnaise has an entirely different consistency from the kind made in a food processor; its texture is richer and more silky and although it's a bit of a bother, it really is worth the effort – the entire family are adamant about this!

1 egg yolk (don't use
  a fresh egg but one
  you bought several
  days ago)
1 dessertspoon
  Dijon mustard
juice of ½ lemon
300ml mild olive
  oil and sunflower
  oil, mixed
salt and pepper

Start by finding a bowl with as narrow a bottom as possible. An old-fashioned glass measuring jug is ideal – what you don't want is a wide mixing bowl.

Put the measuring jug on a damp folded J-cloth in your sink; the J-cloth will stop the jug from moving as you mix, and it is less tiring to mix from a height. Also, the sides of the sink will protect you from the inevitable oil splashes.

Break the yolk into the jug and with a fork, whisk it up really, really well; a couple of minutes spent beating at this stage will make all the difference to the way in which the yolk receives the oil.

Then add the Dijon mustard and seasoning. Mix this all up really thoroughly and then start dribbling in the olive oil very slowly, making sure it's all properly amalgamated before you add the next dribble. Don't be tempted to rush this.

Very soon, the sauce will begin to thicken and at this stage you can start adding the oil a little more quickly. Taste it as you go and when the olive oil taste starts getting a bit strong, switch to the sunflower oil.

Continue until you have a jug full of thick mayonnaise. Finally, add the lemon juice. This will have the effect of thinning the mayonnaise a little, so you may want to add a tiny bit more oil to get it back to the required consistency.

If a recipe calls for aïoli, stir in a couple of crushed garlic cloves at this point.

Nota bene
There is nothing clever about making mayonnaise; you just need patience. However, I have found that results are always better if you don't use a fresh egg and you don't make it on a very humid day. Very occasionally it will curdle (usually when I have rushed the first bit). If it does, break another egg yolk into a clean bowl and begin the process all over again. When you are sure that the mixture has emulsified, add the curdled oil slowly, whisking it in really thoroughly, before adding the next bit.

Mayonnaise will keep in the fridge for two days.

'Caviar'

*'Caviar', or more correctly, lumpfish roe, is a wonderful
standby and I always have a pot of it in the fridge.
Here are three simple ways of using it.*

2 ripe avocados
juice of ½ lemon
150ml crème fraîche
1 pot of lumpfish roe
chopped chives
salt and cayenne
   pepper

AVOCADO AND 'CAVIAR' (SERVES 4)

This may sound dated, but it's rich and
delicious.

   Cut each avocado in half and peel and slice
it lengthways. Arrange on a serving dish and
sprinkle with the lemon juice. Mix the crème
fraîche with some salt and spread the mixture
across the centre of the dish. Sprinkle with
cayenne pepper and chives and decorate
the plate with dollops of 'caviar'.

1 large cucumber
150ml crème fraîche
1 pot of lumpfish roe
chopped chives
salt and paprika

CUCUMBER AND 'CAVIAR' (SERVES 4)

A lighter but no less good version of the
avocado recipe.

   Peel and deseed the cucumber and cut it
into chunks. Add the crème fraîche and arrange
on a serving dish. Decorate with the 'caviar',
chives and paprika. Serve within a couple of
hours or the water from the cucumber will
dilute the crème fraîche.

150g linguine
150ml crème fraîche
juice and zest of
  1 lemon
1 pot of lumpfish roe
chopped chives
salt and pepper

LINGUINE (SERVES 2)

It's important to take trouble over the presentation of this dish: it should look (and taste) elegant.

Cook the pasta according to the instructions on the packet. Gently heat the crème fraîche and lemon juice, season with salt and pepper and pour over the pasta.

Serve the linguine on individual plates and decorate with the 'caviar', lemon zest and chives.

Carrot & Bean Dip

MAKES ENOUGH FOR 6

Don't be put off by the sound of this – it's a version of houmous
that I pulled out of a magazine and I think it's delicious.

3 carrots, peeled
  and sliced
1 tsp turmeric
2 tbsp olive oil
2 tsp cumin seeds
1 garlic clove, crushed
1 tbsp tahini
400g tin of cannellini
  beans, rinsed
1 tbsp lemon juice
salt and pepper

Cook the carrots in boiling water until they
are tender. Drain them, keeping the water,
and put the carrots and all the other ingredients
into a food processor. Whizz the mixture up
till you have a smooth purée and season to
taste. If you think it's a bit thick, add a little
of the cooking water until you get the
consistency you like.

Chickpea &
Coriander Dip

MAKES ENOUGH FOR 6 AS A DIP AND 3 AS A VEGETABLE

*I know this sounds like houmous but because it has one or two extra
ingredients, it somehow turns itself into something quite different.
It can also double up as a vegetable – Skye Gyngell has
a similar version which she serves with lamb.*

400g tin of chickpeas,
    rinsed
2 garlic cloves
2 red chillies
a bunch of coriander,
    including the stalks
a bunch of mint –
    only use the leaves
juice and zest of
    1 lemon
1 tbsp tahini
2 tbsp Greek yoghurt
1 tsp ground
    coriander
1 tsp ground cumin
50ml olive oil
a generous amount
    of salt
pepper

All you have to do is to put all the
ingredients into a food processor and
whizz them up until you have a purée.

Red Pepper Dip

MAKES ENOUGH FOR 8

This dip seems particularly well suited to Le Rouzet, as it is hearty, earthy food. Although it keeps well in the fridge, don't be tempted to freeze it.

5 red peppers
2 red onions,
  roughly chopped
4 garlic cloves ,
  chopped
6 good tomatoes
2 red chillies,
  roughly chopped
a bunch of coriander,
  stalks included
1 tsp ground
  coriander
1 tsp ground cumin
1 tsp mustard seeds
1 tbsp olive oil
1 tbsp balsamic
  vinegar
100ml Greek yoghurt
a small bunch of
  mint leaves
a generous amount
  of salt
pepper

Cut the red peppers in half and deseed them. Cook them at 200°C/Fan 180°C/Gas 6 for 45 minutes with the red onions, garlic, tomatoes, chillies, the stalks of the coriander, the ground coriander, cumin and mustard seeds, the oil, vinegar and plenty of salt and pepper.

When this mixture has cooled down, whizz it up in a food processor with the yoghurt, mint and coriander leaves until you have a smooth purée.

After Dinner Chocolate

MAKES ENOUGH FOR 6

On the occasions when I have completely run out of time and inspiration and I need to produce something sweet, this is my solution. All the ingredients are always in my store cupboard, but use whatever you have: the result is invariably delicious.

200g good dark
  chocolate (70%)
50g hazelnuts,
  roasted and
  roughly chopped
200g mixed peel
  (see below)
crystallised rose
  or violet petals
  (optional)
a pinch or two
  of sea salt

Melt the chocolate in a bowl placed over a pan of simmering water.

Pour the chocolate on to a sheet of baking parchment and then sprinkle it with the hazelnuts, mixed peel, petals (if using) and salt.

Allow to cool and then break up roughly. Serve with coffee.

Nota Bene
I use the excellent orange peel found in all French supermarket, but the mixed peel sold in England is a good substitute.

Burnt Butter Squares

MAKES 16

On a hot afternoon when one craves something sweet, chocolate is often too cloying, so these make a perfect alternative to brownies.

115g butter
230g soft light
  brown sugar
35g demerara sugar
2 eggs
½ tsp vanilla extract
140g plain flour
¾ tsp baking powder
¾ tsp salt
115g walnuts,
  chopped

Heat the butter in a pan over a medium flame and cook it until it turns brown and smells nutty. This should take about 5 minutes but keep a sharp eye on it as it burns very quickly. Pour it into a large mixing bowl and let it cool.

Add both sugars to the butter and beat in a food processor for about 2 minutes. Add the eggs and beat for another 2 minutes. Finally, add the vanilla extract and beat for one minute.

Sieve the flour, baking powder and the salt over the butter mixture and beat to combine. Stir in the walnuts.

Grease and line a small baking tin, about 20 x 20cm. Pour the mixture into it and cook at 190°C/Fan 170°C/Gas 5 for 30–35 minutes.

Remember the mixture will continue to cook as it cools, so err on the side of undercooking; the end result should be gooey.

Cool in the tin. Don't be tempted to cut into squares until the mixture is properly cold. It's impossible to do it without making a terrible mess, and the squares taste better after several hours. They freeze beautifully.

Tuiles

MAKES ENOUGH FOR 8

*These little biscuits are quick and simple to make but transform
an ice cream or a soufflé; they are also another useful way of using
up egg whites. I always have the mixture in the freezer, so it's
really easy to fool people that you have taken a lot of trouble.*

115g butter
85g icing sugar, sieved
85g plain flour, sieved
¼ tsp vanilla extract
2 egg whites

Melt the butter and whisk in the sugar, flour,
vanilla and egg whites. Beat until smooth.

Drop dessertspoons of the mixture,
well spaced out, on to a baking tray lined
with baking parchment. Smooth out each
biscuit until it is an even circle and bake
in a preheated oven at 180°C/Fan 160°C/
Gas 4 for 6–8 minutes or until golden brown.

Immediately lift each one up with a spatula
and drape it over a rolling pin to give it a
good shape.

After a few minutes, the tuiles will have
cooled and you will be able to lift them off
the rolling pin and on to a serving plate.

Brownies

MAKES 20

Adapted from a recipe by Nigel Slater, these are our younger son William's favourite brownies, so much so that he takes a large supply into the office on his birthday; they have become famous amongst his colleagues. If you serve them with ice cream or with crème fraîche, they can double up as a pudding and they freeze beautifully.

250g butter
300g caster sugar
300g good dark
  chocolate (70%)
3 large eggs, plus
  1 extra yolk
60g plain flour
60g cocoa powder
½ tsp baking powder

Line a baking tin measuring about 22 x 33cm with baking parchment.

Cream the butter and the sugar together in a mixer until the mixture is light and fluffy.

Cut 100g of the chocolate into small chunks and put aside. Melt the remaining chocolate in a bowl placed over a pan of simmering water.

With the mixer running, add the eggs and the extra yolk, one by one, to the butter and sugar, followed by the chocolate.

Sieve the flour, cocoa and baking powder into the chocolate mixture and finally stir in the chocolate chunks.

Pour it all into the tin and bake at 180°C/ Fan 160°C/Gas 4 for 30 minutes.

Cool in the tin. Don't be tempted to cut into squares for at least an hour: the mixture is very soft and you will only make a mess.

Apple Cake

MAKES ENOUGH FOR 6

Officially this is a cake, but I sometimes serve it as a pudding with cream or even with custard. As it's very soggy and generally collapses in the middle it never looks quite as good as it tastes.

Cake
butter, for greasing
2 large eggs
1 tsp vanilla extract
120ml vegetable oil
120ml Greek yoghurt
210g plain flour
2 tsp baking powder
1 tsp bicarbonate
  of soda
150g caster sugar
2 large apples,
  peeled and
  roughly chopped

Cinnamon topping
2 tbsp melted butter
50g caster sugar
1 heaped tsp
  cinnamon

Icing
50g icing sugar
2 tbsp milk

Grease and line a 23cm cake tin with baking parchment.

In a large bowl, mix the eggs, vanilla, oil and yoghurt and whisk briefly to combine.

Then add the flour, baking powder, bicarbonate of soda, sugar and apples. Stir thoroughly and pour into the cake tin.

For the cinnamon topping, mix the melted butter, sugar and cinnamon together and sprinkle over the top of the cake.

Bake at 180°C/Fan 160°C/Gas 4 for 35 minutes or until a skewer inserted into the middle of the cake comes out clean.

Cool on a rack and when the cake is completely cold, combine the ingredients for the icing and drizzle all over the top.

Index

About Age Unlimited

Age Unlimited was founded in 2007 by Cathy Gayner and Henrietta Nettlefold to provide support for two groups of people who often feel forgotten: young people growing up with few prospects because of their challenging life circumstances; and the very elderly, many of whom find that in their remaining years, they have become invisible to the wider community and 200,000 of whom are living below the poverty line in this country.

One of the most important aspects of Age Unlimited's work is to bring together these two age groups and encourage them to interact with one another to their mutual benefit. The charity's remit is to raise funds – by means of donations and a varied and personally curated annual programme of literary talks, architectural walks, garden visits, musical evenings and more – with which to support carefully chosen projects set up by other charities who need funds to carry out their work. Thus, Age Unlimited has been responsible for myriad projects aimed at the vulnerable elderly and the vulnerable young, from a coffee caravan visiting isolated pensioners in rural Suffolk, art classes for dementia sufferers, and professional operatic concerts in care homes to homework clubs and initiatives to improve students' literacy and numeracy skills.

Age Unlimited is run on an entirely voluntary basis, with no paid staff. Its Trustees would like to take this opportunity to thank all its generous and loyal supporters over the years.

Cathy Gayner at Le Rouzet

ACKNOWLEDGEMENTS

I am indebted to the following people, without whom this book would never have been written:

Justin Gayner, a wholeheartedly greedy man, a trustee of Age Unlimited and a special nephew. His years of bullying have resulted, finally, in this book and I am profoundly grateful to him.

Henrietta Nettlefold, a dear friend who has always been a joy and privilege to work with. She has slaved away behind the scenes on all the aspects of this book that I have found difficult.

Fiona Duncan, another trustee, who selflessly spent many hours making sense of my recipes and with her husband Andrew, turned an idea into reality in an astonishing act of generosity.

Audrey Nissen, who introduced me to French Provincial Cooking and who was herself an inspiration.

James Murphy, whose evocative photographs have brought my recipes to life on the page. Neither Henrietta nor I are normally at a loss for words, but his generous-spirited approach to this book in aid of our charity, Age Unlimited, has rendered us speechless. Huge appreciation must also go to food stylist Jan Smith, Penny Markham for prop styling along with Props Ltd and to both Lucia Lowther and Sarah Yorke for making the whole experience seamless. More thanks are also due to Lucinda Waterhouse of OKA for her invaluable help.

Alex and Emma Smith, who designed this book with such skill and enthusiasm.

Finally, my debt of gratitude to my family is boundless. Richard, my husband, has patiently eaten his way through endless experiments when I know he would prefer an old favourite such as shepherd's pie. My sons John and William have brought enthusiasm and encouragement and their wives Tessa and Katie have added glamour and happiness to what was a very male environment. I have no words to thank them for the joy they and their children bring me every single day.

—